STEPS TO I

bimh
▲ Publications

STEPS TO INDEPENDENCE:

practical guidance on teaching people with mental and sensory handicaps

A. B. BEST

Foreword: Professor G. B. Simon

First published 1987

© **1987 British Institute of Mental Handicap**
(Registered Charity 264786)

Published by BIMH Publications, Foley Industrial Park, Stourport Road, Kidderminster, Worcs., DY11 7QG

The contents of this book apply equally to people of both sexes, the masculine pronoun being used throughout only for ease of reading.

ISBN 0 906054 61 3

Typeset and Printed by Birmingham Printers (1982) Ltd.,
Stratford Street North,
Birmingham, B11 1BY

CONTENTS

Acknowledgements

The ideas and activities which are included in this book have been compiled from suggestions offered during many visits to longstay mental handicap hospitals, community based adult training centres, and specialist residential centres for people with visual and mental handicaps. I am most grateful to the staff of all these establishments who gave up time to discuss their work with me and allowed me to take photographs, especially those at Christopher Grange in Liverpool, the Elizabeth Gunn Centre in Birmingham, Birmingham Social Services Department's Rehabilitation Unit for the Visually Handicapped, and the staff and residents of Edge View Community Unit, Kinver, who tried out many of the activities.

I would particularly like to thank Professor G. B. Simon, who set up the research project, Bridget Leighton, who made a major contribution by examining the analyses and training activities included in the book, and the care staff who worked with her. My thanks and appreciation also to the editorial staff of BIMH for their support, encouragement, and advice.

Finally I would like to thank the DHSS for the grant which enabled the necessary research to be undertaken, and the RNIB and Sense who have contributed towards the costs of producing the book.

Tony Best

Foreword

This book is the result of a six year study by the British Institute of Mental Handicap (BIMH), sponsored by the DHSS and the RNIB, into the needs of people with mental and visual handicaps, some of whom have additional auditory defects. As part of the study BIMH organised a series of training courses for staff working with people with multiple handicaps of this kind to find out the areas in which they felt they needed help and advice. Hopefully, this book contains the information they are seeking.

The book forms a logical sequel to the BIMH publication *The Next Step on the Ladder: assessment and management of children with multiple handicaps* (Simon, 1986) which is a manual for use in teaching self-help skills and communication to children with mental and sensory handicaps up to a developmental age of about four years. The present publication provides staff and parents caring for adolescents and adults with mental and visual handicaps with background information on how their multiple defects will affect their everyday contact with the world around them. It then puts forward ideas on how the environment can be adapted to enable them to make the greatest possible use of any residual vision they may have and to become confident enough to be able to move around familiar settings with little or no assistance.

One useful way of teaching new skills to people with multiple handicaps is through task analysis which is the method adopted in this book. The main objectives of this method are: to provide guidance on the most appropriate sequence of steps to be used in teaching a particular task; to devise a logical way for people with mental and visual handicaps to tackle the task; and to provide a method of recording the performance and progress of each individual.

Section 5 explains how to draw up an appropriate training programme using this approach. A list of suggested further reading includes books which will provide more information on the use of task analysis and associated behavioural approaches to teaching.

Section 6 of the book comprises a selection of examples of activities which have been broken down into teaching steps using task analysis. These activities have been chosen either because they are useful practical skills essential for independent living, or because they teach the basic skills necessary for carrying out many other activities. Some additional related activities are suggested which offer opportunities to practise the newly acquired skills in a variety of situations. This should make learning more interesting. No doubt readers will be able to find many others to suit the personal requirements of the individuals in their care.

To summarise, therefore, the book is designed to introduce people caring for adolescents and adults with mental and visual handicaps to areas of occupation which those individuals can enjoy, which will make them more independent and more in touch with their environment. It provides sufficient detail to enable carers to move on to developing their own ideas to meet the needs of the people in their care and to make the most use of the opportunities available in a particular setting.

It is estimated that some 12-16 per cent of the people now resident in mental handicap hospitals have visual defects. Many more live at home with their families or in other community settings such as hostels, community units, and group homes. Although some attend schools specially designed to cater for their needs, many attend non-specialist establishments such as adult training and social education centres. It is hoped that staff and relatives will be able to work together to provide a consistent approach to the development of greater independence. This book should be of use to carers in all settings, and should enable them to set up specific programmes of training for the benefit of the people in their care.

It should be remembered that people with mental and sensory handicaps may have emotional problems. Dealing with such problems is a vast subject in itself which is not covered in this book. A number of books and articles on this subject will be found in the list of further reading. It is strongly recommended that psychiatric help should be sought if it is suspected that emotional problems are present. The application of early remedial measures will often enable carers to help individuals overcome difficult problems, and will give them the confidence to cope with other problems that may arise later.

Professor G. B. Simon

SECTION 1

Introduction

What is blindness?

People often think that someone who is blind lives in total darkness and is unable to see anything at all. This is a misconception. Probably 80 per cent of individuals who are classified "blind" have some sight (residual vision) which they can use to perform some daily tasks.

The legal/medical definition of blindness is based on the results of an eye-chart test. If the person being tested can only see the top letter of the chart, his visual acuity score would be 6/60. This means that he can just make out at a distance of six metres what someone with average eyesight would be able to see 60 metres away. A person with 6/60 vision or anything less is classified "blind" but, although his vision is very poor, he is not totally blind.

Ophthalmological tests of this kind require a high degree of cooperation from the person being tested. If that person is mentally handicapped the test results may not give a true measure of his vision, either because he is unwilling to cooperate or does not understand what is expected of him.

The process of "seeing" involves picking up light signals in the eye, and interpreting this information in the brain. Difficulty in seeing arises if either the eye or the brain is impaired in some way. If both the eye and the brain are impaired, as in a person who has both a mental handicap and a visual handicap, the situation is very complex. The eye test result will be of limited value. Further assessment will be needed to discover what use the person makes of his residual vision.

There are various kinds of visual impairment. The effects can result in an overall blurring of images within the visual field; a reduced visual field; patches of reasonable vision within an otherwise poor visual field; or reasonable vision only in certain lighting conditions. This means that the effect of the impairment may be quite specific. For example, one person may be able to walk across a room fairly confidently but be unable to identify objects close to him. Another person may be able to see pictures in a newspaper but will bump into furniture if he tries to cross a room.

To assess a person's functional vision observe him carefully while he carries out a variety of activities. Use different activities to assess the person's near, middle distance, and distance vision. Choose objects that enable you to assess the person's ability to see items of various sizes and degrees of clarity. Also, try to find out if the person can see and follow moving objects, such as someone waving, a moving car, flapping curtains. Such items may be easier to see as they stand out from the background.

Near vision

You can create situations to assess near vision but you can also use many that occur naturally. Suggestions include: putting food on a spoon or fork; picking up a biscuit or cup from a table; reaching for a toy suspended in front of the face; looking at a shiny windmill. Vary the size of the objects (for example, half a biscuit, a whole biscuit, a cup) and the types of background (biscuit on a plain background, half a biscuit on a patterned background) so that you can build up a complete picture of the person's functional near vision.

Middle distance vision

You can assess a person's ability to see objects in the middle distance by using tasks such as kicking a ball, walking up and down stairs, walking to a chair, watching soap bubbles, and following a moving torchlight held 6-10 feet away.

Distance vision

To assess a person's distance vision observe his reaction to objects and events more than 8-10 feet away from him. Suggestions include: watching people enter a room; looking at a dog or horse running in a field; watching television; looking at a house. By asking simple questions (for example: Who is that? What colour is the door? Where is the dog?) you should be able to assess how much the person can see at these distances.

Failure to get a response to middle distance and distance testing may be because of lack of interest in distant objects, rather than a lack of vision. If you suspect this cause use a biscuit, cup of juice, or other favourite item if you consider this more likely to bring about a reaction than other activities.

The information obtained from the results of the person's eye chart tests and your additional observations will help you to decide how to carry out training activities that are appropriate for him, and whether it is necessary for you to make any changes to the surroundings.

What is it like to be blind?

Someone who is blind experiences and learns to understand the world around him in ways that are different from those of a person who can see. The main differences with which he must learn to cope are:

Incomplete information

Imagine a person who is blind standing in the room where you are now. What could he know about the room and its contents? He might be able to feel the floor covering, sense the temperature, and notice any distinctive smell. If he is not deaf he might be able to hear sounds that give clues to its location or purpose. He would, however, be aware of only a small fraction of what you know about the room. Just think of what he would *not* be aware of — colours, shapes, light sources, the position of furniture, pictures on the wall, doorways, other people, and many other aspects that a person with sight would "see at a glance".

If the person who is blind also has a mental handicap, it will be very difficult for him to make sense of the little information he can gather on his own. He may well need help from someone else to understand where he is and what is happening.

Anyone who is blind is severely restricted in the amount of information he can gain from his surroundings. This restriction will affect the whole of his learning. Let me give you an example. If you think of the word "cup" you can probably imagine dozens, made in different shapes, materials, patterns, and sizes. You know that cups can come in a wide range of types. Many of these you will never have touched but will have seen in shop windows, in friends' houses, or on television: your ability to see has enabled you to know of them and be aware of them. A person who is blind, however, will understand the word "cup" to mean only those that he has actually touched, which may be very few indeed. His restricted information will give him a very narrow view of what a cup can be.

The same will be true for almost every word. A person who is blind will grow up with a very limited and incomplete appreciation or understanding of actions and objects.

Different perceptions

Imagine a person who is blind exploring an orange. What aspects of it are likely to be most important to him? Its shape? Its temperature? Its smell? Its sponginess? Its rough texture? These aspects are not the ones that you would probably find most interesting and important when looking at the same orange. For you, the most striking qualities are likely to be its shiny skin and bright colour.

What does the word "horse" convey to a blind person? Probably the sound of hooves, snorting, and neighing; its smell, its smooth or rough coat. These impressions are quite different from the picture of a well-proportioned beast cantering smoothly across a field that the word might convey to you or me.

Speed of observation

Look at a chair. How long does it take you to notice all the main features? One second? At the most, two or three seconds. Now imagine someone who is blind exploring the same chair. How long would it take him? He has to explore each part separately and then try to imagine all the parts fitted together into a whole object. Would this take ten seconds? Twenty seconds? Longer? If he is mentally handicapped as well as blind, he may have great difficulty in puzzling out the way the parts fit together and may take a very long time to decide it is a chair he has found; or he may not succeed at all.

What are the effects of being blind?

The person who is blind will encounter many practical problems which will affect his way of life. For example:

he will not be able to move around as easily as people who can see;

he will not be able to learn by watching other people;

he will not be able to understand some of the things going on around him;

he will not be able to understand the meaning of many words used to describe objects, actions, and situations;

he will not be able to do things as quickly as people who can see.

If the world around him seems too confusing, noisy, and fast moving, the person who is blind may retreat into his own world, spending most of his time in a chair, rocking or talking nonsense, only prepared to indulge in familiar routines. As a result:

he may experience emotional problems resulting from his disability.

It is not possible, in this book, to deal with the treatment of emotional problems. Such problems, however, are very common. Their treatment frequently requires the specialist skills of a psychiatrist. It is recommended that every person who is blind, including individuals who are also mentally handicapped, should be referred to a psychiatrist for advice as soon as any indication of emotional disturbance is suspected.

How can the effects of being blind be lessened?

In order to reduce the effects of being blind, the person who cannot see needs help to learn about the world around him and to become as independent as possible. The ideas put forward in this book are designed especially for this purpose. When using the teaching procedures described always:

help the person to understand what the object or action looks like;

help the person to understand what the object or action is used for;

allow the person sufficient time to explore objects and carry out actions.

Common myths

A common myth is that someone who is blind has a better sense of hearing than a sighted person. This is not true. He may learn to interpret sounds more skilfully, but this skill usually has to be taught.

Another myth is that every person who is blind will have a natural interest in music, or even an innate musical ability. A few do have a particular musical ability, and some are specially encouraged to develop an interest in music. Remember, though, that although a person may seem content to sit and listen to the radio, you must not misinterpret this passive tolerance as genuine interest. The constant sound from a radio can only serve to discourage the person's interest in other aspects of the environment.

Another myth is that a person who is blind will have a very good memory. He may be able to remember where objects have been placed, or to recall clearly events that happened some time ago, but this ability may have been specially developed through motivation and encouragement, rather than being an intrinsic asset. It is likely that a natural ability to remember occurs in people who are blind at about the same percentage as it does in people who are not handicapped.

SECTION 2

General principles of training

Making use of residual vision

A person who is mentally handicapped and blind will probably need training and encouragement to make the best use of his residual vision. In addition to specific training programmes, such as described in Section 5 of this book, there are several simple measures that you should always employ as a matter of course. These are:

Make tasks visually clear

Make sure when carrying out a task that light comes from *behind* the person so there is no light from a lamp or window shining in his face. Glare can make seeing very difficult for a person with a visual impairment.

Avoid working with the person in rooms and corridors which have dark areas where the lighting is poor. This is particularly important if the person is also deaf, as he may be trying to watch your face to help him understand what you are saying.

Present table-top activities on a plain table surface where they can be seen clearly.

Make tasks visually simpler if possible by presenting them in uncluttered surroundings.

Make him look for objects

Expect the person to find and grasp objects on his own. Do not put them in his hands.

Expect the person to use his vision in everyday activities, for example: make him replace his own cup on the tea trolley; expect him to look for and find his own coat.

Allow sufficient time

Be sure to allow the person sufficient time to enable him to look at an object and interpret the imperfect images he sees. He may take two or three times as long as a fully sighted person to recognise the object, even if he is familiar with it.

Encourage him to experiment

Encourage the person to experiment by holding objects at different distances from his eyes, and to each side of him, to establish the positions in which he sees most clearly. He may need to adopt unusual body positions if he is to see objects as well as possible. For example: he may see an object best if it is very close to the side of one eye; he may need to alter his body posture to enable him to see well enough to walk with confidence; he may need to turn his head to one side to be able to paint or crayon.

Moving around

Guiding techniques

A person who is blind, even though he may have an additional mental and/or auditory handicap, may well be capable of finding his own way around familiar environments if taught properly. Before he can be expected to move around independently he will need to become familiar with his surroundings and confident of being able to walk about safely with guidance from someone he knows.

When guiding a person who is blind, walk slightly slower than you would with a sighted person. Make sure you lead him. Have him hold your arm near the elbow and walk slightly in front of him. With practice he will gradually learn that when he feels you move

Note that the person who is blind should hold your elbow and walk slightly behind you.

up or down, or turn as you reach changes of direction, it will be necessary for him to do the same as he follows you. In the early stages, however, you will need to tell him what is about to happen.

Encourage him not to clutch tightly onto your arm, but to hold it lightly as it hangs by your side. If he keeps his elbow close to his side, this will ensure that he follows slightly behind you.

Stairs and steps

Before going up or down stairs or steps, pause. Let the person know whether you are going to go "up" or "down". If he is deaf you can indicate this by jerking your elbow up or down in the appropriate direction. Check that you are both at right angles to the steps. Travelling diagonally across a flight of steps is very difficult if you cannot see them.

It is easier to go up or down stairs or steps if you are both at right angles to them.

It is not necessary to count the stairs. The movement of your elbow, or a change in any handrail that is fitted, should be sufficient to let the person know when they end.

Doors

If it is necessary to guide someone through a doorway or narrow space, move your arm from your side to behind your back, so that the person who is blind is further behind you than usual.

Leaving the person alone

Before you leave a person who is blind alone, tell him you are going. Do not simply disappear. Always leave him in contact with a chair, other furniture, or a wall, so that he

Always leave a person who is blind in contact with furniture or a wall. An open space can be disorienting and frightening.

feels secure. Do not leave him stranded, standing in the middle of a room or corridor without a clear idea of where he is. This would be very confusing and unsettling for him.

Sitting

If you want the person to sit on a chair when you leave him, do not just leave him near to it. Put his hand on the chair so that he can feel it. If you always put his hand on the same part of a chair (the front edge of the seat, the top of the back, or one of the arms) he will eventually be able to work out exactly where to sit down.

If all these guiding techniques are used consistently by everyone in contact with the blind person, he should slowly gain in confidence until walking becomes a pleasant, rather than a frightening, activity for him. An excellent pamphlet on guiding techniques is available free from the Royal National Institute for the Blind.

Using clues

A person who is blind and mentally handicapped can use his senses of hearing, touch, and to a limited degree smell, to provide him with clues that will help him to find his way about.

Hearing

SOUND CLUES

Sound clues can be very valuable if the person can hear. Any sound is a sound clue if it tells the person something about where he is or what is happening. The sound of a washing machine can tell him that he is near the laundry room; the sound of a television may help him find the door if it is just to one side of the television set; the sound of cars will help him judge how far away he is from the road; the squeak of swings should warn him that they are nearby.

Listen to sounds carefully. Walk around wearing a blindfold to identify for yourself sounds which could be useful, and then draw the person's attention to them.

Remember that a person who is blind and deaf will *not* hear any of these sounds. He will not know that the tea trolley has arrived, the minibus is in front of him, you have walked away, or he has been given an instruction, unless someone makes this clear to him. Be aware of situations in which being able to hear is important in order to understand what is going on, especially for a person who cannot see. Make sure that someone helps him know what is happening and what he should or should not do through touch or signs.

HEARING AIDS

The person who is blind and who wears a hearing aid to make the best use of his impaired hearing will have difficulty using sound clues. Sounds will be picked up by the microphone which is usually within a plastic or metal box worn on the chest. The sounds will be heard in the ear, but there will be no indication of where they come from, nor will the relative loudness of near and distant objects be maintained. The person will know only that a noise has been made somewhere. If a number of sounds are present at the same time, this can add to the confusion rather than provide useful information.

It may be possible to help the person make sense of the sounds he hears by training him how to interpret them. Try talking to him about sounds as they occur, or asking him to identify sounds you make. Sometimes, providing the person with two aids, one on each side of the body, can be helpful if he will wear them. Usually, however, a person who is blind and also has a hearing impairment will need to depend more heavily on foot and hand clues.

Touch

FOOT CLUES

Foot clues can provide very useful information to a person who is blind or blind and deaf, even if he has a severe degree of mental handicap. Foot clues often require less interpretation than sound clues or hand clues. It is easier for a person to feel his way along a wall with his foot, or a step down, or the edge of a carpet or mat, than to try to work out where a sound has come from or to remember what type of door knob indicates a particular room.

Someone who is blind can use his feet to obtain information which might help him work out where he is. Encourage him to feel with his feet the changes in floor coverings, slopes, the edge of stairs or steps, and wall/floor edges. Extra clues can be provided by deliberately using different textures for floor coverings, marking doorways with mats, and other simple ideas. These are described more fully in Section 4 of the book.

HAND CLUES

Hand clues can be equally useful for a person who is blind and for a person who is blind and deaf. The person can use his hands to touch objects in his environment which can become landmarks to help him find out where he is. Doors, walls, stair rails, cupboards, door knobs, pillars, furniture, and many more items, can all be used as hand clues.

The person will sometimes be able to identify clues for himself. Watch him walk around to see if he does seem to search with his hands for certain objects or landmarks to help him find his way. If so, encourage him to do so whenever he goes anywhere new to him.

You can do this by showing the person how to develop the technique of trailing. "Trailing" simply means following a wall with an outstretched hand. Teach the person to hold one arm out straight to one side and slightly in front of him with the hand at waist height, and the back of the hand facing forward. As he moves along the wall, his fingers should touch it lightly so that he will be able to detect any landmarks. You can also teach him to hold his other arm across the body for protection in case he bumps into anything in his path.

In this illustration of "trailing" the person is checking her position by feeling for the window and reaching out to find the window frame. Note how she follows the wall with one hand held out in front of her at waist level, while leaving her other arm across her body for protection.

SMELL

Someone who is blind or blind and deaf may use his sense of smell to help him to recognise rooms or work out what is happening. Generally though, this sense is not as useful as hearing or touch. A person who is blind may tend to sniff objects when attempting to identify them. Often, however, the person can identify the object by touch and sniffing has developed just as a habit.

Teaching routes

You may like to begin by first drawing up a list of the routes the person uses often, grading them in order of difficulty according to the number of clues in each one (see Figure 1). This will help you to decide which route to teach first and it will also provide a means of recording the person's progress. The list may also alert you to very difficult routes which could be made easier by the addition of more clues (such as a mat, textured wallpaper, or rearrangement of furniture).

Name:			
Location:			
List of routes to be learned	Not able to manage	Can manage with prompting	Can manage independently
1. From sitting room door to own chair			
2. From sitting room to toilet			
3. From sitting room to dining room			
4. Up stairs to bedroom			
5. From sitting room to front door			
6. From front door to pavement (outside route)			
7. From front door to activity centre (outside route)			

FIGURE 1. Example list of routes to be taught graded in order of difficulty.

GUIDING TECHNIQUES AND CLUES

When teaching a person who is blind to find his way about use the guiding techniques described together with as many types of clues as possible. Identify clues you think will be useful for the person and then take him over the new route many times, pointing out the clues as you go. Let him also use any other clues that he has identified for himself.

You may want to start by teaching him a route from the dining room, for example, to his usual chair. Guide him over the route slowly, putting his hand or feet on landmarks on the way. Once he is familiar with the route, as you reach the last part instead of guiding him hold his elbow or shoulder and let him lead the way. As he gains more confidence reduce the help even more until you need only lightly touch him on the back to encourage him to move forward to the chair. When he can manage the last part of the route without your help, teach him the next to last section in the same way. Continue with this teaching procedure until he is confident enough to manage the whole route unaided.

DIRECTION

Always teach a route in one direction at a time. The return trip, with everything reversed, can be confusing. Do not attempt to teach this until you are quite certain that the person has had sufficient practice in the first direction and can manage it easily.

Special aids

Many aids are available to help people who are blind to move around more easily. Guide dogs, sonic torches, binaural spectacles, and laser-canes all provide help for people trained to use them, but to use them successfully requires a considerable degree of skill and intelligence. A person who is blind and mentally handicapped, and who may also be

For a blind person travelling
in this direction the edge of
the wide open door is a good
mobility clue, but the box left
carelessly on the floor
presents a hazard. If he
walked in the opposite
direction, however, both the
box and the door edge would
be hazardous, especially if the
door had not been pushed
right back against the wall.

deaf, if he is capable of using an aid at all, is more likely to use a white stick or a long white cane. If the aid is to be of real help, the person must be trained to use it properly. An aid that is simply waved or tapped about can become a danger to other people and an unreliable source of confusing information to the blind person. Such aids need *never* be used in familiar surroundings. Instead, encourage the person to use the kind of clues that have just been described.

If it is necessary for the person to walk outdoors, along streets and footpaths, and in unfamiliar buildings, contact the specialist social worker for the deaf-blind, if one is employed by your local social services department, or, alternatively the occupational therapist at your local hospital or health centre. Either of these people will be able to provide you with specialist advice on the best kind of aid for the person to use and may even be able to carry out the necessary training.

SECTION 3

Communication

This book is primarily concerned with people who are mentally handicapped and visually impaired. It can also be used with people who, in addition to these two handicaps, have a hearing impairment. Methods of communicating with people who are handicapped in these ways must be carefully chosen to meet individual needs depending on the nature of their handicap(s).

People who are mentally handicapped and blind

Using your voice

Your voice is the main contact a person who is blind has with you. Is it worth listening to?

Attract and maintain attention

How do you know a person is speaking to you? You know because you can look at the speaker and you can establish eye contact. How do you know he is listening? You may see him nod or shake his head, smile, frown, or acknowledge he has heard you by some other gesture.

How does a blind person know you are talking to him? How does he know you are listening? There are several ways in which you can help to make up for his lack of sight. Use his name in conversation especially when you first begin to speak to him. Say "Yes", "That's right", "Ha-ha" appropriately, as you would during a telephone conversation to make up for responses he cannot see.

Quiet and clear

There is no need to shout when talking to someone who is blind. It will not help him to understand what you are saying, and may make your voice sound unpleasant. Make sure you speak clearly because the person will have to rely solely on what you are saying. He will not be helped by seeing your facial expression, the direction you are pointing, or what you are doing with your hands.

Sound interesting

If we are tired or bored we often try to disguise this by looking interested, but very often our irritation or boredom comes through in our voice. A person who is blind cannot see the way you look and your voice is the main contact he has with you.

Try not to let your voice convey things you do not wish him to know. It is very important that you make sure it *sounds* pleasant, interested, excited, happy, sad, cross, or whatever else you want it to convey. An excellent way to check this is to tape record yourself talking and see if your tone of voice really does express what you are thinking.

Choose words carefully

Try to avoid expressions like "over there", "look out", or "on that shelf". These phrases only make sense if you can see. Instead, try to be more precise about what you mean. Say, "There's a chair near the television", not, "There's a chair over there". If the person is about to crash into something say, "Stop", then explain why. Saying, "There's a vacuum cleaner in front of you, can you find it? Now walk round it. Good!", is much more helpful than shouting, "Look out!".

Think carefully about using other phrases too, such as "behind the chair", "Here you are". A person has to be clear about where the front of a chair is before he can search behind it. This is very easy if you can see, but a person who cannot see will need extra time to find the front of the chair first of all. When you say, "Here you are", what does "here" mean? You may be handing the person an object in your outstretched hand, or there may be an object on a table in front of you. The person will not be sure what you mean unless you tell him clearly, "Here it is, in my hand", or, "It's on the table", and make a noise to indicate exactly where it is.

Look or see

You may be unsure whether to use the words "look" and "see" with someone who is blind. It is probably best to use them when it sounds more natural to do so. A person who is blind "sees" with his fingers, so when you say, "Have a look at this drum", he will know that you mean he should explore it with his hands.

Often the word "find" is a good alternative that you can use. For example, say "Can you find your coat?", or "Find the ball", rather than "Look for your coat", or "Look for the ball".

Add descriptions

It can be very helpful to someone who cannot see if you explain what is about to happen. He may otherwise be unaware of events around him. For example, as you take away his plate after dinner explain, "I'll take your plate away now", or it will just disappear without his realising what has happened. If you are going to turn on the radio, let him know beforehand. Most importantly, if you are going to leave him say something to let him know this, such as "See you later", "I'll be back shortly", or "I'm going into the kitchen to make a cup of tea".

Without this kind of information, the person will have a great deal of difficulty anticipating events and understanding what is happening. This may eventually lead to him ignoring events, rejecting contact, and withdrawing into his own isolated world.

Sometimes it is said of a blind person, "He doesn't miss a thing". This usually means that he uses his hearing well to pick up snippets of information from sounds that might not be noticed by a sighted person. If the person is already listening and making some sense out of his surroundings in this way, try to give him extra descriptions to keep him interested.

Talk with meaning

Someone who is blind may use many words that he does not fully understand. He may talk about a ceiling, waves, a 'bus, without really knowing what they are like. Has the person ever touched a ceiling? Is hearing a wave lap the shore the same as seeing it? Does the person know that a 'bus may have an "upstairs"? As mentioned on page 12, even a common word, such as "cup", may not mean the same to someone who cannot see as it does to someone who can. Try to imagine what the following common words might mean to someone who is blind: fire bell; tea bag; light bulb; curtain rail; bottle of milk; rabbit.

If you are not sure that the person really understands what you say, try to make it clear by allowing him to explore the object with his hands or by demonstrating the action.

You know what is meant by the instruction "Sit down". You have seen many people sitting down and you know what is an acceptable posture. Does the blind person really know what is an acceptable sitting position? Has he been shown the correct position as often as you have seen it? Demonstrate this to him if necessary.

Some expressions, like "March round the room" and "Swing your arms", are difficult to understand and may need to be explained and demonstrated many times. Others, like "Lift your feet up", which really means "Lift your knees up" can be very misleading. Avoid them if possible.

Someone who is blind may talk a great deal although what he says may not always make sense. He may talk not only in order to exchange information but as a form of contact. Just as a sighted person may glance round a room, look at his hands, or gaze out of a window, a person who is blind may talk to keep his mind busy, or establish that he really is there. He may persist with talking simply to force a reaction from other people. This kind of talking may consist of elaborate, but meaningless, repeated words (for example, "gullifilly", "lorrilorri"), nonsense phrases (for example, "up the office", "bell tower ring"), or irrelevant questions (for example, "Have you got a car?", "What's the time?").

If this type of talking is excessive, it will become a problem which will need to be tackled in the same way as speech problems in sighted people. Try to avoid this situation developing by spending time with the person, ignoring his silly phrases, but following up any sensible comments he makes. Sometimes, simply making contact with the person, by touching him or talking with him, may result in a decrease in this type of speech.

Using touch

Touch contact is another substitute for eye contact. Touch the person on the arm or shoulder at the beginning of a conversation to make it clear that you are talking to him. Your touch can be secure and reassuring. It can be friendly, it can be cross, it can be sympathetic. Using touch makes the words you say easier for the person who is blind to understand and also reduces his isolation (see page 26).

People with additional hearing impairment

Even if you are careful to follow the guidelines described above, a person who is mentally handicapped and blind, and who has an additional hearing impairment, may face special problems.

Wearing a hearing aid

A person who is handicapped may strongly resist wearing a hearing aid. There is no easy solution to this problem.

Sometimes it helps if the aid is at first used for short periods only each day. These periods can be increased gradually as the wearer becomes more tolerant of the aid. If you are going to try this approach choose a time for the aid to be worn when there are no unpleasant or distracting noises. An individual music session, using pleasing musical instruments, would be appropriate. Mealtimes on the other hand, which are full of sudden, clattering sounds, would not be suitable.

Sometimes the person may object to having the large plastic earpiece stuck in the ear, rather than to the sounds the aid enables him to hear. If so, try to get him used to wearing the earpiece on its own for a few minutes several times a day. If necessary, you can fasten it to the ear with *Micropore* tape. When the wearer tolerates this, you can introduce sound by adding the leads and the amplifier.

Whistling from the hearing aid earpiece can be distressing, although some wearers seem to ignore or even enjoy it. Whistling is caused either by badly fitted ear moulds or by

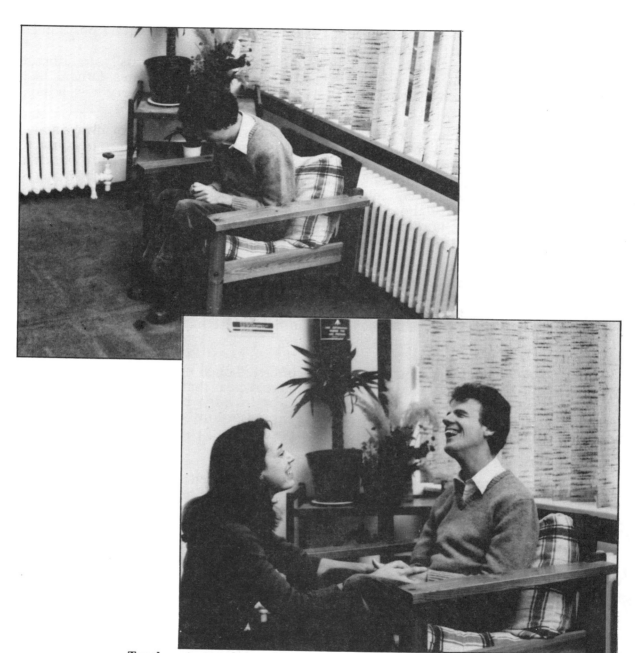

Touch contact can bring a blind person out of his world of isolation.

the volume control being set too high. If whistling occurs frequently, ask your local hearing aid clinic for advice.

Even when the person is used to wearing a hearing aid, he will occasionally misunderstand sentences addressed to him or overhear parts of other people's conversations. This can result in anxiety and confusion. If the person shows any unexpected behaviour always consider the possibility that this may have happened. Reassure him by clarifying what has been said to him or explaining that what he overheard was nothing to do with him.

Using a hearing aid

A person who is mentally handicapped and blind, who also uses a hearing aid, needs special consideration. It is important that some simple guidelines are followed to ensure that the person obtains the greatest possible benefit from the aid that has been supplied.

Daily check

One person should be responsible for checking *every day* that the aid is working. That person should understand the function of each part of the aid and know how to tell whether the battery is charged and the leads, microphone, and earpiece are all in good working order. It is unreasonable to expect *anybody* to wear a broken or damaged hearing aid. It is particularly important that the aid is working correctly if the wearer is blind and dependent totally upon it to maintain contact with his surroundings.

A hearing aid does not enable the wearer to *understand* speech. It simply makes all sounds louder, so that the person can hear more of everything. When trying to understand speech the effect can be a little like trying to understand what someone is saying on a radio that is playing too loudly, or listening to someone on the other end of a very bad telephone line.

Care in use of microphone

Sounds will not reach the person's ear directly, but from the microphone which will pick up all sounds and transmit them through the earpiece into the ear. The microphone, which is usually built into a plastic or metal box, is worn on the person's chest. Try to make sure that it is worn outside the person's clothing or the sound of clothes rubbing across it will block out other sounds.

When you want to talk to the person speak near the microphone rather than into his ear. Speak slightly slower than usual and pronounce words clearly. *Never* shout or speak over-deliberately. The listener may be relying on the natural tone and flow of your words to help him understand what you are saying. Try to find somewhere quiet. Any background noises will be picked up by the microphone and are likely to distract the person from what you are saying and make it harder for him to hear what you say.

Attracting attention

Always alert a hearing aid wearer before you begin to talk to him. Otherwise, you may have spoken several words before he realises you are speaking to him, especially if he cannot see your face. Say his name or touch him on the arm to attract his attention *before* you begin to speak.

It is just as important to let him know when you are about to leave him, so always explain this and make sure he understands. If you do not he may continue to talk to you after you have gone, and he will become confused and anxious if you do not reply.

Using signs

Sign systems

No sign system has yet been specially designed for people who are blind as well as deaf. Some of the signs in the *British Sign Language* (BSL), which was originally developed for deaf people of normal intelligence, are suitable for use with people who are also blind and mentally handicapped. The *Makaton Vocabulary*, which comprises 237 signs extracted from the BSL, is the system most commonly used these days with people with such multiple handicaps. Even so, some of the signs involve complex hand movements in the air which can be very difficult to learn without sight.

If the BSL does not contain suitable signs for actions or objects which you and the person in your care use frequently, it will be necessary for you to devise suitable signs that you will both understand. Such signs will enable the individual to make his needs known to you and to understand what you require of him. They can be made up from any definite hand movement, such as: clapping hands, rubbing the tummy, tapping the back of a hand, clasping hands, rubbing the chin, brushing the fingers up and down the palm of the other hand, tapping a fist in the palm of the other hand, rubbing a shoulder, tapping a thigh, and so on. Make sure that other people in contact with the person also know the meaning of the signs you teach, so that he will be able to make his needs known to them in your absence.

Selecting signs to teach

As well as the hand movements that have been suggested in the previous paragraph you can select other signs to indicate favourite toys or activities: swing, rocking horse, trampoline, large ball, coloured torch, rocking chair, sandwich, bath, spinning top, tickle. Signs for some of these are included in the *Makaton Vocabulary*, but others you will have to devise yourself.

Make sure that the signs you teach will be useful to the person you are teaching and will help him to communicate. There are opportunities for communication in most activities. You can encourage the person to use the sign for "please". You can teach him signs for the names of things he enjoys, and eventually he will be able to use the appropriate sign to ask for a specific item. If you, and others around him, consistently use signs before routine events take place he will learn to anticipate what is about to happen; for example, that he is to be taken to the toilet; lifted up; given a drink; tickled; washed; given a biscuit; or that he is to have his coat put on and go out.

Teaching signs

The aim of teaching signs is to help the person who is deaf and blind to make more sense out of his surroundings. Signs will enable him to communicate, anticipate actions, make decisions, and control events.

Signs can be taught by a process of conditioning — the close association of a sign with an action or object. It is best to try to teach all signs in everyday situations where they will have real meaning rather than in isolated teaching situations. It is also advisable to limit teaching to only a few signs at a time. Extra signs can be taught when the first few have been mastered.

If you are going to start teaching the person some signs, begin by selecting ones that can stand for everyday routines such as washing hands, having a meal, or getting a drink. In the early stages of teaching let the person first feel, for example, the sink, plate, or cup and then guide his hands through the movements of the sign. Follow this immediately with washing hands, serving a meal, or pouring a drink. When the person is familiar with the meaning of the sign, you can start to use it *before* the event. Guide his hands through the movements of the sign. He should then go, with help if necessary, to the appropriate place, that is, the sink, or dining table. In this way the person will gradually learn to anticipate events.

Suppose you want to teach someone who is deaf and blind a sign he could use for the phrase "Can I have a drink?". A suitable sign would be tapping the lips with the fingertips of one hand. The best time for you to begin teaching this would be when a drink would

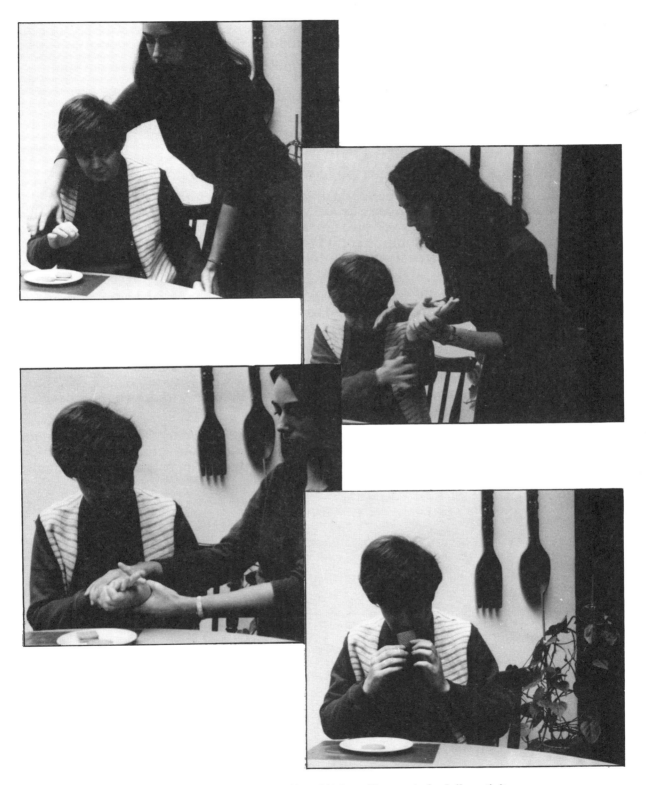

Teaching the signs for "biscuit" and "please" as part of a daily activity.

normally be given, rather than in special teaching sessions. You will need first to offer the drink and then demonstrate the sign. You could use the following sequence.

1. Let the person feel the cup with a little liquid in it, then take it away from him.

2. Hold his right hand and move it so that the finger tips tap his lips several times.

3. Immediately put his hands around the cup and let him drink the liquid.

4. Take the cup away and put a little more liquid in it.

Repeat stages 1 - 4 until the person has had sufficient to drink.

You will need to repeat the sequence on many occasions before the person realises that making the sign results in being given a drink. When he understands this he will eventually make the sign himself as soon as you give him a cup. In order for him to learn to associate the sign with a drink, it is very important: (1) that the sign is *always* followed by a drink; and (2) that everyone in contact with him follows the same procedure *every* time he is given a drink.

The person may eventually use the sign spontaneously when he feels thirsty, but this may not happen until the sign has been used routinely at drink times for quite a long time.

Developing the person's communication skills may well result in him taking more interest in the daily routine and in his surroundings. Communication will help him begin to make more sense of the world rather than experiencing it as a meaningless series of actions. He will feel more secure as he learns to anticipate what is about to happen to him. He will be less confused and anxious, and less likely to become withdrawn or to develop severe behaviour problems.

The section on "Communication" in *The Next Step on the Ladder* (Simon, 1986) gives additional information on ways of improving both verbal and non-verbal communication in children who are multiply handicapped. Many of the ideas suggested are equally applicable to adults.

SECTION 4

The living environment

Adapt or not?

There are many ways in which you can adapt buildings in order to make life easier for people with mental, visual, and possibly auditory handicaps. This Section of the book identifies variables which you need to consider if you wish to make your setting provide the best possible living, training, and learning environment. The amount and type of adaptation you undertake will depend very much on the individual handicaps and needs of the person, or group of people, using the building.

Before making any major, permanent changes consider carefully the ability levels of the people in your care and your aims for their future. A building which has been adapted until it is very "special" will certainly be helpful to them while they are living in it — but if they become too dependent on special "support" features how will they fare if they move to another setting?

The ideas that follow indicate the extremes of each variable. You will have to decide on the balance that is appropriate for your setting. Inevitably, the amount of money available will influence the extent of any structural changes you make. You will, in any case, need to be very certain that you will need such adaptations on a longterm basis before embarking on them.

The emphasis, therefore, is on more flexible, non-permanent adaptations, for example, rubber mats rather than textured floor tiles, that can be added when their support is needed but can be removed when they are no longer needed.

Variable 1: sound

Sounds can be a very valuable source of information for a person who is blind but is able to hear. They can tell him *who* is in the room, help him find out *where* he is, and tell him *what* is happening in the room, hallway, corridor, or outside. They can also provide a source of interest and contact with the environment. How can you make the best use of this variable?

Echoes and areas

A blind person needs to hear sounds that are clear if he is to be able to work out what they are and where they come from. If sounds echo this may be very difficult for him. Carpets and curtains "deaden" extraneous noises and make it easier to hear useful sounds. Room dividers, which also help to prevent echoes, can be used to create "sound areas" within a big room. If you use these carefully the person should find it easier to gather useful information from listening to the sounds around him.

In a large room, try to arrange the furniture and carpets to make areas that sound different, such as: a partitioned-off area in the corner with carpet and a circle of chairs; an open area with vinyl floor covering and few items of furniture; a large "busy" area with carpets, tables and chairs, and activities.

What you do will depend on the space available, but if possible try to provide a variety of experiences, not just the easiest one! Whatever else you do, try to provide a small, carpeted area (about 9' x 9') in which the person can sit in "his own chair". Studies have shown that people who are mentally handicapped and blind may be greatly influenced by the size and sound of the area they sit in, and that they may find this size the most "comfortable".

Arrange furniture to create small areas.

Direction

Sounds can help someone who cannot see know where he is in a room in relation to the furniture, walls, or doors. The most useful sounds for this purpose are the fixed sounds that occur almost all the time. Such sounds are particularly valuable if the room is large. Try to ensure that one or two sound sources of this kind are provided. For example, you could use a ticking clock (provided it is not so loud that it is irritating), a tropical fish tank (even though it cannot be seen by the person it provides a distinctive sound), a tinkling mobile, or a bead curtain across a doorway. Other sounds from nearby rooms or outside the window can also be helpful, such as a washing machine, flushing toilet, or passing traffic. A radio or television, when on, can indicate direction but these should *not* be left on all the time. A pet, such as a budgie or a gerbil, can be another useful sound source. You will be able to think of many more to suit your particular setting.

Whatever you choose it is important that the person who is blind is taught to listen to the item and that he can make sense of it. Take him to the object that makes the sound and explain what it is. Let him feel it. Encourage him to find it himself. After a while he may be able to judge whether it is "nearby" or "a long way away". He may be able to describe the sound to you and how he uses it. Even if he cannot do this he may still be helped to know where he is by the sound without realising that it is providing him with a clue.

Environmental sounds

Sit in the room where the person who is blind spends much of his time, with your eyes closed, and listen. You may be surprised by how much noise there is. You will probably be able to hear sounds that come from outside the room and outside the building. Some will be interesting and will give you information (such as the tinkling of tea cups, a clock chiming, or rain beating on the windowpane).

Ask yourself, is the noise level pleasant, or is it overpowering? Are there so many noises that you begin to feel confused and just want to sit in a corner and try to ignore them? Is there a useful variety of sounds providing an interesting "picture" of what is happening? Is there any conversation going on? Hearing people talking close by can be pleasant, interesting, and reassuring. Remember this and, when in the presence of someone who is blind, make a special effort to start conversations, or describe things that have happened, or that you have done.

It is *not* good to have a radio or television on all the time. These mask many useful and interesting sounds and are likely to result in the person not bothering to listen for them. Use them only when they are likely to offer something of interest to the person.

To summarise, then, the ideal sound environment will have *variety*, both in types of sound and degrees of loudness. Remember, silence can sometimes be golden, even for people who are blind.

Variable 2: walls

"Trailing", as described on pages 19-20, is a skill which you can teach to someone who is blind which will help him find his way about. The person learns to hold out his hand slightly in front of and to the side of him, with the back of his hand facing forward and his fingers lightly touching the wall at waist level. As the person follows the wall he can feel for clues that will tell him where he is and what is coming up next.

What sort of clues will be helpful? And, what can be confusing or dangerous?

Special clues

Apart from on flights of stairs or steps a handrail is rarely necessary for someone who is blind, especially in a familiar environment. If the person is just beginning to learn to find his way around, you can help him by fixing an easily-felt strip of material (such as rope, textured wallpaper bordering, sponge draught-excluder, or velvet ribbon) along a wall at hand height to mark out a route, say, between a sitting room and the toilet. If the doors on the route are usually kept closed, stick the material on the doors also.

In long corridors, or in complex buildings, use a distinctive wall covering to identify a wall that can provide an important clue; for example, the wall opposite the sitting room, the wall leading to the junction of three corridors, or the wall which continues on both sides of a door in a corridor. The wall covering should contrast with other wall surfaces. You could use wood-chip, flocked, or hessian wallpaper, and leave all other surfaces smooth.

Tactile "labels", which stand proud of the surface and can be identified by touch, can be added to doors to make them easier for the person who is blind to recognise. Wooden

Tactile "labels" can be used consistently on coat hooks, personal belongings, doors, and furniture to help the person find his own property.

or plastic shapes are suitable for this. If several people who are blind use the building each one should be allocated a shape of his own. The shapes can then be used to identify each person's coat peg, chair, bed, wardrobe, and bedroom door. When the person finds his own shape on any item he will be reassured by it and know that the item is his.

The heating pipe, mirror, telephone flex, and door frame all provide useful clues to help the person understand where he is.

Remember, though, that with all these ideas it will be necessary for the person who is blind to know what they mean. You will have to take him to the clues, explain what they are and what their purpose is, and allow him to feel them with his fingers. You may need to do this many times, but eventually such clues should help the person find his way around more easily and know when he is in the right place.

Natural clues

Often special clues are unnecessary. Many features which occur naturally can be used as clues. The best way for you to identify these is to walk along a route wearing a blindfold, seeking them with your hands and feet. You may find: various kinds of door handles which can be used to identify different rooms and entrances; door frames and window sills that stick out slightly and give good warning of doors and windows; and metal protective strips, which are sometimes fastened on inside walls, can indicate a corner. Notice boards and pictures, which may be very striking visually, are usually too high up to be found easily by hand and so are of little use.

The chair, windowsills, step, and bricked edge to the path provide "natural" hand and foot clues.

Remember that if you encourage the person to explore walls thoroughly with his hands, he will eventually come across light switches, electric sockets, and, possibly, fire alarm points. If you judge this to be too dangerous, concentrate on hand trailing only at waist level where such hazards rarely occur, and encourage greater use of foot and sound clues.

Some features can be a nuisance. Fire extinguishers, for example, are often placed too high to be found by a trailing hand, but are the same height as the face. Partly open windows and doors that protrude into a pathway can be dangerous. Refuse bags left against a wall or on a pavement are too low to be found by hand, but can easily cause an unpleasant accident. You may want to ensure that these dangers, and many others like them, are removed. Alternatively, you may feel it is worth pointing out such hazards, and helping the person in your care to learn to cope with them.

A dangerous hazard
for a blind person.

Dangerous doors

An extra word about doors. Half open doors are very difficult to detect by listening or by feeling. They can cause nasty cuts to the face and should *never* be allowed in a building used by someone who is blind. It is important, therefore, for everyone in contact with a person who is blind to be alert to the danger and ready to close, or fully open, doors that they find ajar. Self-closing fastenings on doors are helpful as they ensure that doors are always kept fully closed. If you are choosing a door closure make sure that the mechanism works slowly and does not snap back quickly, catching the heels of the person walking through the doorway or jamming his fingers.

Variable 3: floors

As with walls, you can add many ingenious features to help someone who is blind to find his way around, but beware of making the person too dependent on the help you provide.

Stairs and steps should be marked and it is also helpful to indicate where a room begins, particularly any leading off a hallway or corridor. A metal strip across the bottom of the door frame is sufficient for this purpose. A very distinctive smell, sound, or item of furniture may be enough to enable the person to recognise which room he is entering.

You will have to decide how much information to provide, dependent on the person's individual needs.

Floor surfaces made up of a mixture of textures can help a person who is blind find his way around. In this illustration the tiled surfaces indicate "open" areas in the centre of a large foyer, the wood block square warns of the junction of two corridors, and the carpeted strips indicate direction and lead down the various corridors.

Mats

One very useful piece of equipment is a non-slip mat. This can be used in front of a doorway to indicate a room off a hallway or corridor, to warn of a door across a corridor, or to mark the junction of two corridors or pathways. It can also be used at the top and bottom of stairs. A series of mats can mark a route across a large area. One particular advantage is that a mat can be easily moved around to provide help where it is most needed at any time.

Suitable rubber mats come in a variety of styles. If choosing a mat make sure that it will not slip, and that it does not have raised edges that can be tripped over. Make sure that it feels quite different from the floor surface on which it is to be placed. Some car mats and plastic carpet-covering strips are also very suitable. Flimsy woollen or nylon mats, which are often used in bedrooms and bathrooms, are *not* suitable as they are easily kicked aside and tend to "ruck up", thus becoming a hazard for someone who cannot see.

Surfaces

You can provide permanent floor marks at important or hazardous points in the building if you think they will be needed for a long time. They are particularly valuable at the top and bottom of flights of stairs and steps, but can also be used elsewhere. Again, the idea is to provide a floor surface that will feel markedly different from its surroundings. Suitable materials include cork and ceramic tiles, nylon "grass", textured rubber industrial floor coverings, and wooden floor boards and blocks. Apart from these special features try to provide a variety of floor coverings throughout the building which will help the person who is blind to make the best use of foot clues to recognise where he is.

Hard surfaces, produced by vinyl floor coverings or tiles, can be used in hallways, entrances, and corridors. They reflect sounds and so provide warning of other people walking nearby. However, because they reflect sounds they sometimes create echoes, especially if used in long narrow corridors. Be careful not to use these materials if echoes are produced, as this would create difficulties for a person who is blind who would not be able to establish where the sound was coming from. In sitting rooms and bedrooms carpets, as well as being "normal", are warmer and more comfortable. They absorb sound and make it easier to pick out useful sounds. Dining rooms probably need to be a compromise between hygiene, clear foot clues, and a good sound environment. An easily washed carpet is perhaps the best surface.

Stairs and steps

Provided the person with mental, visual, and auditory handicaps has no marked physical disability he should have no particular difficulty coping with a straight flight of stairs or steps once he knows they are there. There is no reason to exclude them from his environment, nor to exclude the person from an environment which contains them. It is useful to indicate the top and bottom of the flight, perhaps by means of a contrasting floor texture as already described. A gate can be put at the top of the stairs if you think there is a very real danger that the person might fall down them, but such accidents are very rare. A firm handrail, at a suitable height, is important and you must show the person where it is and teach him how to use it. It must be continuous so that it can be followed along landings as well as up and down the stairs.

A solid continuous handrail with contrasting posts to warn of changes of direction or gradient can help people who cannot see to find their way around independently.

Wide stairs and steps are much more difficult for the person to negotiate than narrow ones as he will have to depend on the handrail only as a guide and will be unable to touch the wall on the other side. Irregular steps such as in a spiral staircase, or a single step into a room, are more difficult to cope with. It is probably best to avoid these if possible.

Stairs and steps outdoors can be a hazard. Make sure that suitable warning clues are provided. A handrail which starts horizontally just before the top of the flight, should be added if at all possible.

Mobility training circuit

Outdoor paths, if properly designed, can encourage people who cannot see to walk on their own. The easiest surface for the person to identify is usually smooth concrete, tarmac, or cement, with a clearly defined edge (not a drop) to the grass or soil at the side. If you use paving stones make sure they are carefully laid to avoid any hazardous ridges between slabs which could cause the person to trip over.

Sometimes a "mobility circuit" can be provided following a route round the outside of a building and through the surrounding grounds. If this is to be used for training, then a variety of surfaces can be incorporated. A loose surface, such as gravel or sand, is much more challenging than a firm one. Paving stones can be spaced out within a turfed area, but again care must be taken to ensure that they are not raised above their surroundings.

Special mobility circuits. Paths can be clearly defined by raised edges or grass borders.

A very advanced, winding route could be marked only with a low fence a few inches high. A very high degree of mobility skill would be required to negotiate this without "losing" the route or being tripped up by the fence.

Variable 4: furniture and equipment

Furniture

People who are visually handicapped can learn to cope with most standard items of furniture. There is little you can do to make these easier to use. The way you arrange the furniture, however, is important.

**Arrange furniture to provide the person with clues that will help him to feel his way
along a direct route between the door and his own easily identified chair.**

A person who is blind will use furniture not only as the designers intended, but also as a support or a clue. He will undoubtedly bump into furniture more often than people who can see. Cupboards, bookcases, or dressers, especially if used as room dividers, need to be sturdy enough to withstand occasional knocks from someone who weighs perhaps twelve stones or more. If there is a possibility of an accident being caused make sure the items are securely fixed so that they cannot be pushed over. It is preferable to fix items by means of brackets attached to the ceiling or a wall. Fixing items to the floor can result in protruding metal bolts or brackets which can be dangerous.

Items such as low coffee tables should not be used. They are difficult for the person to find except by banging into them. This can cause a painful bruise on the shin, or even a fall.

Arrange it!

Arrange furniture in a way that provides a balance between a pleasant appearance, good mobility clues, and practical convenience. Arrange some items to provide landmarks across the room. Also, try to use the furniture to divide large spaces into small areas. The person who is blind can then keep track of events occurring within one area at a time more easily. Arrange chairs in small circles of, say, five or six. Use settees, cupboards, and other large items to create partitions between areas. Remember, a large empty space is difficult for someone who is blind to negotiate unless there is a strong clue to give him a sense of direction (for example, the sound of cups on a tea trolley).

Move it!

Although a person who is blind will use furniture as landmarks and to provide him with mobility clues, it is important to rearrange it once or twice a year. Do *not* make changes more often than this or the person may become insecure. A person who cannot see tends to rely on routine to make sense of the world. If encouraged, this can result in overdependence on that routine, until eventually the person will react strongly against change, including anything new or different in his environment. This can become an extra handicap as the person will avoid exploration, will lack initiative, and will refuse to take part in many daily activities.

You can help the person to avoid becoming overdependent on routine by moving items in his environment so that he has to think more about his surroundings. Each time you make any changes show the person round the room systematically and explain the differences to him. Look out for any difficulties he may have in finding his way afterwards and for any reluctance to move out of his chair. If you see any of these signs spend extra time getting him used to the new arrangements.

Open spaces

If you are lucky enough to have sufficient space, try to keep just one large empty area specifically for encouraging movement and exploration without injury. This area should be large enough to run in. It must *always* be kept clear of obstacles. A gym or hall in which the floor slopes up to the walls would be ideal, but you can manage with a much smaller area. If possible, add a three foot wide border of contrasting floor covering to warn of the edge of the room. Any blind person using the room will feel more confident when moving around quickly if this warning clue is provided. Make sure that activities in the area are carefully supervised.

Equipment

Many small items of equipment can be introduced to make daily living easier.

In the dining room, for example, *"Dycem"* non-slip mats on the table and straight sided plates may be of particular help to someone who can see neither his food nor his spoon.

In the bathroom a number of simple changes can make life easier. For example, hanging a towel on a large peg near the side of the hand-basin is much easier than using a towel rail, especially if the towel itself rather than a loop can be hung over the peg. Using push-in towel holders can be easier still. Single sheets of toilet paper that can be pulled out separately from their holder are easier to manage than lengths of paper torn from a roll. Suction pads or secure soap dishes, perhaps even built-in, enable the person to find the soap more easily and are very much better than easily moved soap bowls or shallow recesses in the hand basin.

The range of equipment available is very wide. A good source of information is a catalogue of special aids such as the one produced by the Royal National Institute for the Blind. Help can also be obtained from the specialist social worker for the deaf-blind employed by Social Services Departments. These staff are specially trained in techniques for rehabilitating people who are blind. They may well be able to advise you on the selection of appropriate small items of equipment according to individual need.

Variable 5: lighting, decoration, and furnishings

As explained at the beginning of this book many people who are called blind are not totally blind. Some can see light, colours, windows, door frames, or moving objects. Others have very poor vision but enough to be able to cope with everyday situations, even if they are sometimes rather clumsy. How can you improve the environment to make life easier for these people?

Lighting

Good lighting is very important. The amount of light in a room can dramatically alter the extent to which a person with poor vision can see. Good lighting is not the same as bright lighting and, although a good overall illumination is necessary, lighting should not be so strong that it causes discomfort.

Try to provide lighting that is slightly brighter than usual but is glare-free. This applies to all areas used by the person with poor sight, including hallway, stairs, landing, and bathroom. Make sure the corners of rooms are also well lit. Provide table- and standard-lamps to give extra lighting for the person if he is able, and wants, to see small objects, but check that the shades prevent glare.

Glare presents a person with poor vision with an even bigger problem than poor lighting. It causes great difficulty to someone with cataracts. Glare results from inadequately shaded lights, sunlight shining through dirty windows, and strong single light bulbs. You can usually prevent glare quite simply by providing adequate lamp shades, fitting low-power fluorescent tubes, keeping windows clean, and fitting blinds or curtains to shield bright sunlight.

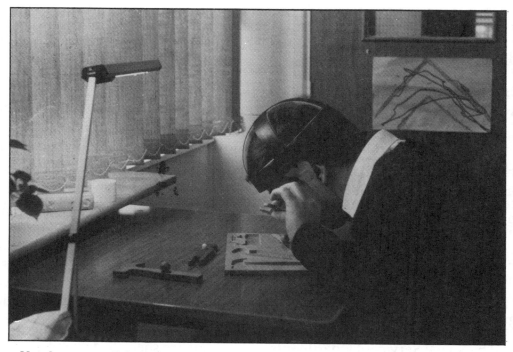

Note how excess light and glare from the window has been reduced by vertical blinds. Most light is reaching the table from the room lights behind the person, but extra glare-free lighting is provided by the table lamp. Notice how this lamp is positioned well above the person's head so that it does not cause discomfort, and that it prevents an area of shadow that would otherwise be created by his head and shoulders.

Light sources can provide mobility clues. A person may be able, for instance, to follow a line of lights along a corridor or across a room. Make sure that light clues are used carefully, and *always* in conjunction with other clues, such as the sound of footsteps or the position of the furniture, so that the person does not miss important warnings of hazards.

Careful positioning of lights in the centre of corridors and over doorways can provide useful mobility clues for people with partial sight.

Decoration

Decoration is also important. The colours used on the walls and ceiling can affect the brightness of a room. Avoid dark colours, especially on ceilings, as they reduce the available light. Do not use fussy, multi-patterned decorations. These may confuse someone who does not see clearly.

When decorating, the best principle to follow is contrast. Use plain, contrasting colours so that objects stand out clearly from the background and features such as corners and doors can be more easily located. Paint door frames in a colour which contrasts with walls and doors so that they stand out clearly. You can even paint the corners of rooms and the skirting boards in a strong contrasting colour if you think it may help. Small items, such as doorknobs and light switches, will also be easier to see if they are in a contrasting colour. If they cannot be painted, use coloured insulating tape to highlight them.

The photographs on the next two pages illustrate how paying attention to colour details can benefit someone with poor vision and assist in enabling the person achieve the greatest possible degree of independent mobility.

Furnishings

Select furnishings, such as carpets and curtains, carefully. Remember the setting in which they are to be placed. If the setting has a multi-coloured, patterned carpet, choose

 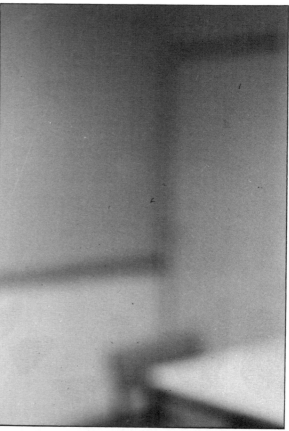

The photograph on the right simulates the effect of partial sight. Note how the wooden strip along the wall and the door frame, which are both painted in a constrasting colour, provide an aid to someone who cannot see their position clearly. The floor covering, which also contrasts with the walls, offers additional help.

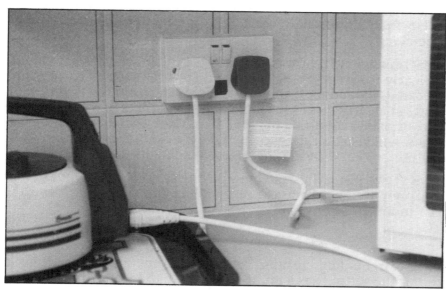

The high contrast in the right hand plug makes it much easier to locate by someone with poor vision as it stands out much more clearly from the background than the white plug.

Even in this dark area the contrasting white strip on the edge of each stair tread, and the clear contrast between the stairs and the wall, makes the task of walking up easier.

plain furnishing fabrics which will offer a good contrast. Do not choose furniture which is the same colour as the floor covering or walls.

You can make it easier for the person with poor sight to see an open doorway between two rooms by selecting different floor coverings for the two areas which contrast well with each other. A metal or wooden strip across the doorway can also help, but make sure it will not cause the person to trip. Mark the edge of the tread of all stairs and steps with a white strip which is either fixed or painted on.

Try to maintain contrast throughout the building in respect of the decorations, furniture, and equipment used. For example, at the table choose plates that are a different colour from the food placed on them, and place them on table mats in a contrasting colour so that they can be seen more clearly.

SECTION 5

Training approaches

Introduction

This Section is intended to help you to draw up a training programme for someone who is visually and mentally handicapped, and who may have other sensory or physical handicaps. It will give you some starting points by providing analyses of various kinds of activities that can be tackled by people who cannot see. You will need to select some of these activities and add ideas of your own in order to make a balanced and appropriate training programme for the person in your care.

What daily activities can the person join in? What recreational activities might he enjoy? What skills does he need to help him understand his surroundings and be interested in them? Ask yourself these questions. You may find that the answer is that he can carry out the same activities as a sighted person but that he may need help, or he may need to learn a different way of doing them, perhaps with some special aids.

The tasks that have been selected for inclusion are a logical sequel to those contained in *The Next Step on the Ladder* (Simon, 1986). They are divided into four categories: Art and Craft; Mobility; Housecraft; and Food and Drink. All of them are designed to teach skills which will be of practical use in the daily routine. Each task has been analysed into small steps. This will enable you to identify the parts of the task that the person can already manage by himself. Having done this you will be able to see where to begin teaching.

At the end of each of the four categories is a list of suggested "Related activities" which you might like to try. These can provide varied opportunities to practise specific skills and so make learning more interesting. For example, making sandcastles involves the same skill of filling and carrying a spoon that is used in putting sugar in a hot drink.

Assessment

A person's training programme should be based on the findings of an assessment of his capabilities and needs. Such assessment can be carried out using several assessment scales.

Very few scales have been developed specifically for use with people who are blind or partially sighted. The *Maxfield-Buchholz Scale of Social Maturity*, although American and developed in the early 1950's, is probably the scale most widely used with people with visual handicaps.

It may well be helpful, if you have not already done so, to also assess the person in your care on the *NSL Developmental Assessment Scale* contained in *The Next Step on the Ladder* (Simon, 1986).

Other scales commonly employed to assess people with mental handicaps can be useful, but they must be used with care as many of the items included require the use of good vision and so may be inappropriate. Sections from the *Progress Assessment Charts*

(Gunzburg, 1973) the *Portage Guide to Early Education* (Bluma, Shearer, Frohman, and Hilliard, 1976), the *Balthazar Scales of Adaptive Behavior* (Balthazar, 1981), the *AAMD Adaptive Behavior Scale* (Nihira, 1974), and the *Developmental Checklist* from *Helping the Retarded* (Perkins, Taylor, and Capie, 1981) have been used successfully. You will need to select the scales you consider most appropriate depending on the individual impairment, abilities, living situation, and needs of the person in your care.

The analyses

The analyses contained in this book, which begin on page 62, have three purposes:

to provide you with guidance on the sequence of teaching steps;

to present a logical way for someone with a visual handicap to tackle each task;

to provide you with a method of recording an individual's performance, and his progress on each task.

Each of the analyses describes a simple method of carrying out an activity that has been found to work with people who are visually and mentally handicapped. It does not describe the only way. If a person can already complete an activity using a different technique, he should not be made to change. If he is experiencing difficulty in carrying out or learning a task, however, it may be worthwhile trying the approach described.

Each analysis sets out the criteria for successful completion of the task, and offers comments which give practical advice on how best to undertake the necessary teaching. A score chart of four columns is provided for recording the stage the person has reached on each step. These are:

1st column. Not able to cope
    This step is judged too difficult or dangerous for the person to cope with and so it is done for him.

2nd column. Has hands guided through
    This step is too difficult for the person to do alone but he is being taught to do it by having his hands held and guided through the action.

3rd column. Can manage with prompting
    The person still needs some help to carry out this step but not as much as in Column 2. The help will usually be physical guidance, but it may be a gesture or a word of explanation.

4th column. Independent
    The person can carry out this step without any help.

Drawing up a training programme

You will want to draw up a training programme to meet the specific needs of the person in your care. To do this use the following procedure.

1. Establish what the person can already do by completing a number of appropriate assessments such as the ones suggested above.
2. Select a small number of tasks which you think the person will be able to learn and which would be useful to him.
3. Use the detailed task analyses provided in Section 6 (or draw up some of your own) to identify the steps which the person can already do.
4. Teach the remaining steps in the order given, completing the relevant columns to provide a record of the person's progress on each task.

Starting the training

You may think at first sight that some of the descriptions in the analyses sound very complicated and require the person's fingers and hands to be placed in complex positions. When you try them out, however, you will find this is rarely the case. Before you attempt to teach the person, go through the analysis of the task you are going to teach, step by step, and try it yourself, preferably wearing a blindfold. You will then know exactly what the activity consists of and will be aware of how best to guide the person through each step.

When teaching an activity begin with only a few steps at a time, so that the person will not be overwhelmed. Completing the score chart of the analysis of the task you are teaching will help you to identify the steps you should do yourself and the ones that the person can do with help or by himself.

Related activities

The related activities listed at the end of each of the four task categories provide opportunities for practising the basic skills that are being learned. Practising will enable the person to strengthen skills which he has recently acquired and will allow him to use these skills in more complex activities. Select related activities for the person in the same way that you choose the main tasks; make sure they are appropriate and useful for that person.

The person will probably find the activities you choose enjoyable and rewarding in themselves. Even so he may need other rewards, such as praise, a sweet, or a drink, to motivate him to undertake some of them at first. Again, choose rewards which are suitable for the individual you are teaching and that you know he will find pleasing.

Expanding the training programme

The activities in this book are only intended to provide you with a starting point. They should serve to illustrate the wide range of skills and activities that can be taught to people with multiple handicaps. The types, combinations, and degrees of handicaps and abilities of people who are multiply handicapped are so diverse that each person's needs will be different from anyone else's. It is up to you to compile a training programme which will meet those individual needs. This will almost certainly mean adding to the list of tasks and related activities and drawing up the necessary task analyses and score charts.

Carrying out the training

Establishing contact with the environment

Before you can begin to teach someone who is blind the skills he needs to become more independent, you will have to make certain that he is aware of his environment and what is happening around him and to him. This is particularly important if the blind person is very severely mentally handicapped. A person who is severely mentally handicapped and who has very small remnants of vision and hearing may not be aware that he can see or hear. If so, then you will have to stimulate him appropriately, for example, by teaching him to link the images he receives with his eyes to the objects that are around him. Remember to allow him plenty of time and to encourage him to touch and explore the objects.

If no effort has been made to involve him in what is going on around him, or in what is happening to him throughout the day, the blind person may show no reaction or interest. You will have to try to stir him out of this situation by creating an environment which is interesting and which he can understand. It will help if you establish a daily routine which is simple, consistent, and regular so that gradually the person will begin to anticipate what is going to happen next. Involve the person in appropriate activities, such as the ones described in this Section, and explain them to him as you go along.

Encouraging movement

If the person in your care is physically handicapped it is particularly important that you encourage appropriate movements, as advised by a physiotherapist. The exercises likely to be recommended will be designed to:

> extend joint movements;
>
> strengthen muscles;
>
> provide experience of different body positions, such as horizontal, vertical, and reclining;
>
> make use of soft, hard, cold, and warm surfaces;
>
> encourage fun through water play; and
>
> provide movement on rollers.

The advice given by the physiotherapist will be specific to the person's individual needs and abilities.

Positioning

Different activities require the person to adopt different positions. Before you begin an activity with him, make sure that he is in the best position for it. He may need to sit, with a back and head support; he may need to lie down flat, with some clothing removed; he may need to lie on his stomach, supported by a wedge.

This person has adopted a very close working position in order to see the task more clearly. Encourage experimentation to find the best position for each person for the activity being undertaken.

Make sure the environment is appropriate also. Think about the activity you are going to attempt. Could sounds, or people moving around, cause any confusion? The person may seem to be oblivious of everything happening around him. Even so, present the activity with as little distraction as possible.

Encouraging use of the five senses

The activities that follow can be used to help people establish contact with and an understanding of the environment. They are suitable for you to use with people who are mentally handicapped, blind, and deaf. They are therefore primarily tactile and rely largely on the sense of touch.

Many people with severe handicaps, however, have some residual vision or hearing and, almost certainly, an ability to taste and smell. It is important that you make as much as possible of all these five senses.

Vision

If you think there is a possibility of some vision being present, even if the person does not seem to use it, consider the visual impact of what you are doing. For example: hold up a garment so that the person can look at it before putting it on; move your fingers in front of his face before you move them down to tap the back of his hand.

Hearing

Even if you are not sure that the person has any useful hearing always use sound when approaching him in order to try to avoid him being startled. For example: say his name clearly before touching his arm to let him know you are there; make a noise with an object, a hairbrush for instance, by shaking it or tapping it on the person's wheelchair, the floor, or a table before you touch the person with it; use your voice while carrying out activities to add interest — sing as you rub the person's skin, make a "whooshing" noise as you pull material across his legs, talk to him to explain what you are doing.

Taste

Provide the person with a wide variety of foods and drinks so that he can experience the different flavours. In this way you may be able to find out what he most enjoys and what he dislikes. This can help you to decide on appropriate rewards.

Smell

A strong smell can be used to stimulate a reaction, so think about the different smells of the items used in the activities you choose. If you hold the items close to the person's nose you may be able to tell from his response whether he likes certain smells or not, for example, suede, rubber, onion, lemon, mint. Again, this information can help you to decide on appropriate rewards. Remember, most materials smell more strongly when they are warm.

Smells can also provide the person with information. For example, if you always wear the same perfume or after-shave he may learn to recognise you, even though he cannot see you.

Touch

For someone who cannot see touch is perhaps the most valuable of the senses. He needs to develop the use of his hands to collect information. You can help him develop this skill. Place his hands on an object and give him time to explore it with his fingers. You may need to guide his index finger at first to help him explore the object thoroughly.

This person is exploring teapots. One hand is being gently guided over the important features of a teapot while the other holds it steady.

You can see and identify an object at a glance. Someone who is blind, however, has to put together a series of sensations in order to identify an object. With some objects it can make the task easier if you give him a fixed point from which to explore. For example, to explore a teapot, first let the person hold the handle with one hand. Then, holding his wrist, move his other hand round the nearest side to the spout and back again. Then move his hand round the far side of the teapot to the spout and back again. Finally, guide his hand across the top and the base in turn, and back again. Having explored the object thoroughly in this way the person must put together all the impressions he has gained to make up a picture of what a teapot is like.

Before you begin any activity with a person who is blind move his hands all around the area in front of him so that he knows what is there. Make sure his hands are in contact with the surface at all times. If they are raised into the air, the person will have no idea what is beneath them.

At meal times, for example, move both his hands along the edge of the table, then bring them together and move them away from him to the mat, plate, and cutlery. Then guide them nearer to the centre and to the sides of the table before bringing them back in front of him. If he can hear, you can encourage him to name some of the objects as he feels them, or you can name them for him yourself. In this way you can help him to find out exactly what is on the table. You may need to show him how to explore the table many times. Eventually, however, he will learn how to do it himself.

Always encourage the person to use both hands when exploring, starting with the hands together and then moving them apart. Otherwise he will not know what is between his hands. For example, if he holds both ends of a length of rope, he will not know how much rope there is, or whether it is tangled up or neatly coiled.

A small object, which can be held within the person's hands, is easier for him to understand than a bigger one. Encourage him to explore it thoroughly with both hands. With a larger object, like the teapot described earlier, one hand will have to hold on to the item while the other moves around it. The person will then have to put together, in his mind, all the separate pieces of information he has gained to form an impression of its shape and size.

It is very important for you to teach the person to use both hands together in any manipulative activity, such as putting pegs in a board, making shapes with *Plasticine*, threading beads on a stick, or playing in sand. Using one hand or finger as a "base" or fixed point can be particularly helpful in the early stages. For example: one finger can stay on the last peg placed in a peg board while the other hand moves to pick up the next peg; one hand can hold the centre of a piece of *Plasticine* while the other pulls out the ends into the required shape.

Using touch with someone who is very severely or profoundly handicapped

Awareness of touch comes only through movement. It is barely possible to feel a completely stationary hand when it is touching you. You are only likely to become aware of it from movement which creates either variations in pressure on the skin or a sensation of motion across the skin. You can provide the person in your care with experience of a wide range of types of touch, varying from light brushing to hard pressure.

Ensure that *nothing* you do causes pain. Once you are certain of this you can vary the speed and the intensity of your touch. Always remember though that you are trying to find the most gentle stimulus possible that will create awareness and bring about a response.

Touching activities can include:

pinching	slapping	flicking
pulling	scratching	tapping
pushing	stroking	tickling.

You can vary each of these activities by doing them: on bare skin; through clothes; and when wearing a variety of gloves of different texture (leather, rubber, cotton).

Begin by trying the activities on the person's palms, forearms, and thighs. Once he is used to this you can move to more sensitive areas, such as the ears, neck, tummy, and the soles of the feet.

There are many variations you can try using different types of touch and different parts of the body. For example, you could begin with a scratching movement made with bare fingers on the back of the person's hands, then on his thighs. You could repeat the sequence wearing leather gloves. You could then repeat the whole series two or three times more. The whole session should last for about 10 minutes.

Repetition *in* a session is important, as is repetition *of* a session. Both lead to familiarity which results in the person feeling more secure, anticipating what is to follow, and understanding what is happening.

Blowing and sucking

As with touching, introduce variety to make activities more interesting. For example, use: a hair dryer; a bicycle pump; and a vacuum cleaner. Use hot and cold air alternately. Blow: on the same spot; in circles; up and down the body. Suck clothes and skin with the vacuum cleaner.

People with sensory handicaps often enjoy the sensation of the vibration produced by machines with motors if they are held against the skin. Let the person get used to the equipment and its vibrations. When he is accustomed to this you can let him feel the air being sucked in and blown out.

Materials

You will be able to find a great many materials to use in activity sessions which will provide a variety of textures. Examples include: silk, wool, greaseproof paper, cotton wool, sponge, plastic/rubber sheeting, velvet, leather, corduroy, tin foil, fur, flannel, foam rubber, suede, and carpet.

Use them in interesting ways such as:

fasten various materials on to a frame mounted around the wheelchair or suspended near the person so that he can feel them with his hands;

fasten materials on to a board and encourage the person to explore the board with his hands;

wrap the person in long pieces of material and then carefully roll him out of them;

tie the person in a large piece of material and, with someone to assist you, swing him gently from side to side, up and down, backwards and forwards, fast and slow, and in a circular movement;

brush or rub pieces of material on various parts of the person's body, using varying degrees of pressure and different speeds;

You can use two materials at once; for example:

rub one of the person's arms with fur while you roll crumpled paper over the other — the contrast might help to make the person more aware that something unusual is happening;

put small pieces of different fabrics into a plastic box, guide the person's arm or leg into the box, help him to move it around and feel the different textures. (Alternatively, hide a toy in the box and help the person to find it. Or for a change, use sand, water, lightly inflated balloons, or wood shavings.)

Skin sensations

Many substances can be put on to the skin or rubbed into it. They can provide a range of contrasts as do the materials already described. Most of the substances listed here result in a smooth sensation, but some have a more dramatic effect. Before you begin, try to let the person know something is about to happen so that he will not be startled.

Examples of suitable substances are:

salt, orange juice, ice cubes, hand cream, shaving cream, talcum powder, chalk, baby oil, sand, and raw egg.

As well as the sensation of touch, you can choose substances that make use of the sense of smell. You can either:

rub these directly on to the skin; or,

impregnate a cloth with the substance and rub that over the skin.

Suitable strong smelling substances include:

eucalyptus, *Vick*, garlic, perfume, lemon juice, and vinegar.

For a change, you could use aerosol deodorants and perfumes that can be sprayed on to the skin, or different brands of talcum powder and hand cream which have a variety of scents.

Touching, and being touched, are two different experiences. As well as using the substances yourself with the person, therefore, encourage the person to rub them into his skin surface himself, for example, by rubbing his hands together, or rubbing his chest with one hand.

Signs and gestures

You may be able to use signs and gestures as indicators of what is about to happen. You could use them to warn the person that you are about to touch him, or that he is to be given food, moved, or changed. Signs you could use include: blowing on face; rubbing ear; tapping chin; rubbing thigh; clapping hands; and scratching elbow.

Simple signs such as these will help you to communicate with the person and will help him to make his needs known to you. This will help him make sense of the world and make his contact with people less confusing and more meaningful.

A description of techniques for introducing communication, including signs and gesture as well as spoken language is given in *The Next Step on the Ladder* (Simon, 1986). See also the advice given on teaching signs on pages 27-30 of this book.

Noting responses

Watch carefully for any response to an activity which may indicate interest. The person may respond by a hand or eye movement, by squirming, or by vocalising. You can record the response on a chart such as the one illustrated in Table 1. If you do this regularly you will be able to see whether the response changes with time to become more noticeable or more definite; for example, shoulder squirming may become a firm hand movement such as pushing away.

Selected activities	Types of response						
	Pushes away	Withdraws hand	Increased tenseness	Smiles	Laughs	Reaches out	Other
1. Gently stroke back of hand with fingertips							
2. Blow cool air from hair dryer on face							

TABLE 1. Chart for recording responses to selected activities

Do not be surprised if the response does not always indicate pleasure. The person is likely to find your intrusion on his solitude uncomfortable at first, and he may well show an angry response. This discomfort, however, is not the same as pain or fear which would gain nothing. A certain degree of discomfort can be helpful. For example, if you place a cloth over the person's face, he may respond by a movement to remove it; if you stick *Plasticine* on the back of his hand, he may respond by moving his hand to shake it off.

In addition to a response to the chosen activity, if you carry out your programme regularly each day the person may learn to recognise what is about to happen and may react in anticipation. It may be something he can see, hear, or feel which tells him what is going to happen and produces the response. For example, if he sees a jug of water that is to be poured over his hand he may move his hand away; if he hears the hair dryer he may realise it is going to blow air over his face and he may turn his face towards it. You can help him learn to anticipate by consistently using signs before carrying out the various activities.

Teaching new skills

How to teach

As a person who can see you learned each skill, such as brushing your hair, partly by watching others and partly by doing it yourself. As you became more competent you checked your efforts in the mirror, or compared them with those of other people. This told you if you had brushed your hair correctly. Someone who is blind cannot learn by watching other people. He is unable to see what he has done and so he cannot monitor his efforts or make comparisons.

If you want to teach someone who is blind any new skill (such as a simple assembly job, pouring a drink, or fastening a coat), you will have to show him the correct way of carrying out the task. To do this, stand beside or behind him and, holding the back of his hands, move his hands through the necessary actions. You will probably have to do this many times. Think how often you, as a child, saw people eating before you could use a knife and fork properly!

When the person begins to anticipate the actions you can start to withdraw your help and let him attempt some parts of the task on his own. Do this by holding lightly on to his wrists rather than his hands, and later his forearm, giving him time to move his hands through some parts of the task himself. Gradually you will be able to let him do more and more until he is finally able to carry out the task unaided. When he is confident enough, you will not need to hold on to him. A sign or gesture or, if he can hear, a verbal instruction will be sufficient to let him know what is required.

As an example, take the activity of hand washing. Stand beside the person, holding your hands over the back of his. Guide one of his hands to the tap. Place his fingers over the tap and twist his hand round to turn it on. Move his other hand across the back of the basin, touching the surface all the way, to find the soap.

At the same time, if he can hear, tell him what is going to happen. Use short, simple sentences, such as "Let's find the tap. Good. Now we are going to turn it on. Turn it with me. That's right. Now this hand is going to look for the soap. Move it along the basin like this".

If the person cannot hear, guide his hands through the sign for wash (that is, rub both hands together) and then continue with the sequence of actions. As he becomes more proficient, as he should do after a number of demonstrations, you can reduce the amount of help you give. Let him feel for the tap on his own, or look for the soap himself while you hold lightly on to his wrist or forearm.

Another way of helping him learn is to let him feel other people as they perform a task. For example, let him hold your hands while you brush your hair. Let him feel your hair before and after it has been brushed. This will help him to understand what is expected of him when he does the task himself.

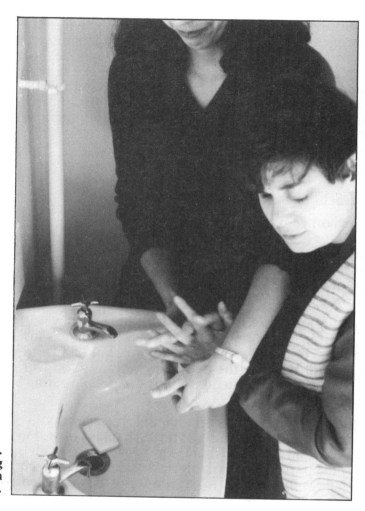

**Hands on hands.
Demonstrate skills by guiding
the person's hands through
the actions.**

Making learning successful

Any person learns more quickly and enjoys learning more if he is successful. This is especially true of someone who is blind, who probably faces many frustrations every day. You can ensure he achieves success by breaking down tasks into small steps and teaching him just one step at a time.

If you want to learn a foreign language, you do not start by attempting long sentences. You begin by picking up odd words, and then phrases of several words. If you are learning to drive a car, a good instructor will first show you the correct driving technique and then teach you this one step at a time.

This step by step approach is very suitable for you to use with someone who is handicapped. You will need to break down each task you wish to teach into small steps and teach the person one step at a time, usually starting with the last step so that the person always completes the task successfully. These procedures, called task analysis and backward chaining, are clearly described in *Helping the Retarded* (Perkins, Taylor, and Capie, 1981). The example activities in Section 6 of this book have already been broken down into teaching stages. However, if the person you are teaching has difficulty learning a stage you may need to break it down into even smaller steps.

As the person learns each new step, praise him. Let him know that he has done well. He will then think that learning is pleasant and he will continue his efforts to be successful. A person who is handicapped, especially if he is blind, may have difficulty appreciating that he has completed a task satisfactorily. It is, therefore, very important while he is learning that you reward him *immediately* every time he is successful. Praising him by saying "Well done" may be a sufficient reward, but he may need something more tangible — a hug, a tickle, a piece of fruit — as well. The techniques of selecting and giving appropriate rewards is described in *Helping the Retarded* (Perkins, Taylor, and Capie, 1981) and some ideas for use with children who are multi-handicapped are given in *The Next Step on the Ladder* (Simon, 1986).

Creating a good learning environment

Whatever you set out to teach, learning will be more enjoyable and more successful if the teaching takes place in a good learning environment. There are several principles which you need to follow to achieve this. Some have already been mentioned but they are restated briefly here to provide a quick checklist.

Remove distractions

There may be various distractions in the room in which you are working, or even outside the room. Those at a distance can create an interest which distracts the person's attention from the task in front of him. Those nearby can cause clutter so that it is difficult for the person to concentrate on the appropriate objects. There are three kinds of distractions.

1. VISUAL

If the person has some residual vision, ensure that the background to the task itself and the surrounding area are not distracting. A patterned wallpaper can make an object in the foreground difficult for the person to see. Bright splashes of colour near the work area may be visually attractive, but they may detract attention from the task in hand. Objects close by, not connected with the activity, can cause confusion.

You can reduce visual distractions by choosing a place to work in which is as uncluttered as possible and by removing any unnecessary objects.

2. TACTILE

Tactile distractions, such as small objects and interesting textures, may interfere with the concentration of someone who is totally blind. Small irregularities on the surface of the table, the frayed ends of an apron, or a piece of torn cardboard on a box, can be enough to distract attention from the task.

You should always be on the lookout for things that might be interfering with the person's concentration.

3. SOUND

Someone who can see will find it easy to anticipate and locate sounds and can quickly ignore them if they are not associated with the task in hand. Someone who does not see or hear clearly will find this much more difficult. The sounds he hears may be a source of interest, confusion, or curiosity to him which will interfere with his concentration.

Try, therefore, to use a room which is quiet so that the person will not be distracted by the sounds of traffic or of other people who may be nearby.

Check table height

When working at a table, make sure the table top is not too high or too low. The person should be able to reach objects comfortably without hunching his shoulders or arching his wrists. If he is blind and using touch he must be able to rest his forearms on the table while he explores with his hands.

You will probably be able to keep the person interested in the task longer if he is comfortable.

Keep objects in a frame

Place a frame around the objects you are using to prevent them from dropping off the table or moving out of arm's reach. A box with low sides or a tray with a straight edge may well be sufficient. If you are working on the floor, objects can be placed within an old tyre or inner tube.

Remember, the person you are teaching will soon lose interest in an object if he can no longer see or reach it.

Clear the work area of distractions and place the objects to be used within a tray or frame so that the person does not lose them.

Explore the whole area

Make sure the person knows what is in front of him by allowing him, or making him, explore the area with his hands. Otherwise, he may not realise what is there. Refer to the section on using touch (pp 50-52) for advice on how to do this.

Explore objects

If you are helping a person who is visually handicapped to explore objects, you must decide whether to place yourself behind or beside him in order to guide his hands, or opposite him where you can guide his hands but also watch his eyes to see what he is looking at. A person can sometimes feel uncomfortable if you lean on him from behind, "crowding" him, with your arms on both sides of his head.

Give the person time to explore an object thoroughly, enough to allow repetition of the finger movements as he may not discover all the features of the object the first time he examines it.

Use clear descriptions

Make sure that the words you use convey your meaning clearly. Use words that the person knows and say them distinctly in a normal voice. Do not shout. Make your voice sound pleasant and do not let any irritation or boredom show through. If the person is blind avoid expressions like "this one" or "over here" unless you can indicate exactly what you mean by making a sound with the object or letting the person touch it.

Replace objects

If you move an object in the room or on the table top, think carefully about where you replace it. If you do not put it back exactly where it was, you will create an extra difficulty for someone who cannot see. You will have to decide whether moving the object will distract him from the task he is attempting, or whether he has reached a stage at which it is appropriate to make the task more difficult by making him find the object in its new location.

Coping with mannerisms

Reasons for mannerisms

Often, someone who is blind will develop mannerisms, such as rocking, eye-poking, headbanging, picking, and finger-flicking. Experts are unable to agree on the reasons for this. It is possible that the person develops mannerisms:

because he is bored;

as a reaction to stress or anxiety, which then develops into a habit;

because he finds them pleasant activities, carried out because there is little or nothing else of interest in his surroundings;

because at first they help to relieve a pain in the ear, eye, or other part of the body, but then become habits done without thinking.

The person who is blind will not have seen how other people behave. He will be unaware of how peculiar his mannerisms appear to sighted people. Interested readers will find a discussion of the possible reasons for the development and maintenance of mannerisms in *Self-Injurious Behaviour* (Gardner and Murphy, 1985).

Effects

Very occasionally habits of this kind can result in damage. Eye-poking, for example, can result in an infected eye. Once established, such habits can cause the person to seek inward stimulation rather than to look for and join in activities with other people that are going on around him. Apart from the adverse effects on the person himself, other people are often irritated by seeing him indulge in habits which make him appear more handicapped than he really is. Again, refer to Gardner and Murphy's (1985) book for further information.

Breaking the habit

Mannerisms are very difficult to remove and doing so requires a great deal of consistent hard work. You will not be able to stop the person's mannerisms by saying, "Stop that rocking", or, "You are poking your eye — stop it!". The person may stop for a very short time, but will then continue as before.

It is possible that your comments could even make the situation worse — by drawing attention to a behaviour that the person comes to realise is bound to result in him being given extra attention. Once he has learned this he is likely to increase the frequency of his mannerisms so that he gets attention more often. Alternatively, your remarks could cause the person anxiety, which again might result in increased manneristic behaviour.

As with any habit, the person will often do it without realising. Probably the most effective way of changing this type of behaviour is by means of behaviour modification techniques. This means that you must give the person attention, praise, and rewards, at times when he is *not* doing the mannerism. In order to do this, provide him with some interesting activities and encourage him to keep himself occupied with them when he is on his own. This will give you opportunities to praise and reward him and he will learn that this more acceptable behaviour pleases you and results in attention. You *must* remember, however, to make contact with him frequently while he is occupied, and not to ignore him because he is quiet. When he does begin the mannerism stop him straight away with the minimum of fuss and preferably without making any comment. For example, if he starts eye-poking tap his hand sharply but not hard enough to hurt him, or if he starts rocking poke his shoulder gently. These actions will alert him to the fact that he is doing something you do not like.

It is essential, if a behavioural programme is to succeed, for it to be carried out consistently. Try to ensure that, as well as you, everyone else in contact with the person adopts the same approach at all times following a pre-arranged and agreed plan.

It will probably not be possible to continue the programme to reduce the mannerism throughout the whole day. If so, it is best to begin by tackling the problem at one particular time every day, such as lunch time, or while the person is engaged in a particular activity. Do not expect quick or dramatic changes. It may take many months to bring about any improvement.

SECTION 6

Activities

Introduction

This Section provides a few examples of specific activities that someone who is blind might want to carry out. Each one has been analysed into components to give you an idea of the order in which to teach the various parts of the activity.

The examples are divided into four categories: Art and Craft; Mobility; Housecraft; and Food and Drink. At the end of each category is a list of related activities. These offer opportunities to practise the skills being learned.

The analysed activities chosen as examples illustrate how basic skills are used in many everyday activities. They also show some of the special difficulties that someone who is blind may face when learning a new skill. Use them when you want to teach these activities to someone who is blind, or as a guide to refer to when you want to break down a different task into a number of teaching steps. Use the related activities to provide the person you are teaching with opportunities to practise what he has learned in a variety of situations. This will make learning more interesting and more useful for him.

When you are used to this approach to teaching you will be able to draw up a list of activities which you and your colleagues think would be particularly useful and appropriate for the person in your care. You will then be able to plan which activities you are going to teach first, analyse each one into its component parts, and begin teaching. If you find that the person you are teaching has particular difficulty with any teaching step, consider whether it is possible to break down that step into even smaller components.

The books by Gardner, Crawford, and Murphy (1983) and Perkins, Taylor and Capie (1981) are particularly useful in helping you to decide on the order in which to teach the parts of an activity and assisting you in your attempts to undertake the task analyses.

CATEGORY 1
Art and craft

Task analyses

The example task analyses and related activities in Category 1 can be used to provide practice in manual dexterity and touch. These skills are very important as they are used in many everyday activities. They also offer practice in identifying different shapes and textures, and encouraging listening. Also, the tasks and activities described can provide a useful source of leisure time occupation.

TASK ANALYSIS 1
Pulls *Plasticine* apart

Goal: Can divide one lump of *Plasticine* into two pieces

If the person does not understand or enjoy this activity, his hands may be limp and he will not be able to squeeze or pull. It may help if you encourage him first to hold the *Plasticine* firmly above the table. The action can be used in many everyday activities, such as removing lids from containers. To provide variety, let him practise the actions required using biscuits, bread, bananas, or lego blocks which are fastened together.

STEPS	Not able to cope	Has hands guided through	Can manage with prompting	Independent
1. Locates piece of *Plasticine*				
2. Holds *Plasticine* in both hands				
3. Squeezes *Plasticine* with both hands				
4. Moves hands apart pulling *Plasticine*				
5. Stops pulling when *Plasticine* tears				

Notes

STEP 1.   This activity will be easier if at first the *Plasticine* is already rolled into a sausage shape. Let the person explore the *Plasticine* so that he knows it is in one piece.

STEP 2.   Place the person's hands so that the index fingers are touching when he holds the *Plasticine*. He will then be able to feel when the *Plasticine* has come apart as his fingers will no longer be touching.

STEP 5.   Encourage the person to feel all round both pieces of *Plasticine* so that he understands what he has done.

TASK ANALYSIS 2

Puts *Plasticine* together

Goal: Can combine two pieces of *Plasticine* to make one lump

This skill is generally taught after the person has learned to pull *Plasticine* apart. The same action is used in claywork and pastry-making.

STEPS	Not able to cope	Has hands guided through	Can manage with prompting	Independent
1. Locates and holds one piece of *Plasticine* in one hand				
2. Locates other piece with other hand				
3. Places second piece on top of first piece				
4. Pushes palms together to stick pieces				
5. Checks and stops pushing when two pieces are stuck together				

Notes

STEP 1.　Each piece of *Plasticine* should be small enough to fit into the palm of the hand so that fingers can be wrapped completely round the ball. This provides the easiest position for checking if the pieces have been squeezed together.

STEP 4.　Think about how the pieces *feel* when put together. They may feel as if they are combined but still *look* like one piece on top of another. At first accept this as adequate.

STEP 5.　When the person has practised joining the pieces together encourage him to persevere until he makes them into one ball or sausage shape.

TASK ANALYSIS 3

Sticks with glue

Goal: Can apply correct amount of glue from glue pot and stick glued surface to base

Before using a glue pot and paste brush introduce the idea of applying glue using glue pens, bottles of gum, and glue sticks which will not spill or run too fast. Allow the person to apply the glue with his fingers in the early stages, as this will help him to understand how to spread it all over the required surface. Let him practise with stiff card, plastic tiles, or polystyrene squares. Do not use paper until later as it tears easily and is difficult to feel. The spreading movement can also be used when spreading bread or cleaning a table top.

STEPS	Not able to cope	Has hands guided through	Can manage with prompting	Independent
1. Identifies outline of item to be stuck				
2. Holds glue pot in one hand				
3. Holds paste brush handle in other hand				
4. Puts paste brush in pot				
5. Lifts paste brush out of pot				
6. Lets go of glue pot				
7. Finds surface to be glued using free hand				
8. Locates edge of surface with index finger				
9. Places paste brush on edge of surface next to finger				
10. Slides paste brush across top of surface				
11. Moves paste brush down surface to spread glue				
12. Locates pot and returns paste brush to pot				
13. Relocates glued side of item				
14. Turns item so glued side faces downwards				
15. Locates base with other hand				
16. Puts glued side of item on base				
17. Presses down on glued item				

Notes

STEP 2.   It is helpful to keep the pot on the table close to the surface to be glued. Non-spill paint pots are particularly suitable. Teach the person to hold the pot round the top with one hand for stability, and also to help with Step 4.

STEP 4.   The person may find it easier if he puts the first finger of the hand holding the pot across the top of the pot. He can then use this finger as a guide while he slides the brush down into the pot.

STEP 7.   Place the item to be glued within a frame. This can be a wooden or metal mask, a photographic printing frame, or even a steep sided tray. This will help to hold the item still and provide an outline in which to work.

STEP 8.   You will need to guide the person's hand initially.

STEPS 9, 10, 11.   This technique is suitable for square or rectangular shapes. Initially, the paste is put along one edge and then spread by a series of strokes down the paper. Do not try to teach this technique until the person is used to putting paste on the surface in a random manner.

STEP 17.   Encourage the person to press down with one hand in the centre of the item and to smooth it out if necessary with the other hand, moving it from the centre outwards in different directions.

TASK ANALYSIS 4

Weaves cane through uprights

Goal: Can weave a piece of cane through uprights

This analysis does not cover the skills needed to thread uprights, join new pieces, or trim ends as they are all probably too advanced for the person you are teaching. If the person masters the technique of weaving, however, and you think he can learn the more advanced skills, he should be helped to do so as making cane objects can be a very satisfying leisure activity.

Throughout this activity, the person's fingers should always be kept close to the cane being worked.

STEPS	Not able to cope	Has hands guided through	Can manage with prompting	Independent
1. Holds cane and upright with one hand				
2. Finds next upright with second hand				
3. Moves hand on cane forward to upright				
4. Twists cane round upright				
5. Presses cane down				
6. Moves second hand along cane pulling clear of other uprights				

Notes

STEP 1.   This will usually be done with the left hand. The purpose is to keep track of the upright which has just been used, as well as to control the cane.

STEP 2.   This will usually be done with the right hand.

STEP 4.   In this manoeuvre, the second hand has to move the cane round the upright in the correct direction. It is often useful for both hands to keep in contact with the upright as this is being done. This ensures that only one upright is involved.

STEP 6.   This movement is carried out while the first hand holds on to the cane and upright. The shorter the cane, the easier this step is. The cane can be pulled towards the body to move it clear of the other uprights.

TASK ANALYSIS 5

Threads rope through hole

Goal: Can thread rope through a hole

In this activity, the rope is put through a hole in a piece of card or a plastic ring. If you do not have a rope that is firm enough, the task can be carried out with a stick instead. The action learned can later be used for threading necklaces or bracelets as a leisure occupation, or for threading shoe laces.

STEPS	Not able to cope	Has hands guided through	Can manage with prompting	Independent
1. Finds and holds the end of the rope in first hand				
2. Finds the hole with the second hand				
3. Moves first hand towards second hand until end of rope is near the hole				
4. Finds hole from other side with second hand				
5. Puts first finger of second hand through the hole from the inner side				
6. Locates end of rope with first finger				
7. Pushes rope through the hole with first hand				
8. Grasps end of rope with second hand and pulls it through				

Notes

STEP 1.   Show the person how to hold the rope with one finger touching the end so that he knows eactly where the end is.

STEP 2.   You can help at first by holding the card or ring so that the person can use one hand to hold the rope, and the other to find the hole. Later the person can learn to locate the item himself and then find the hole.

STEP 3.   If one finger has been placed correctly alongside the end of the rope, this finger can feel for the hole.

STEP 4.   The second hand is now moved right around the card or ring to find the other side. You can help at first by holding the item as in Step 2.

STEP 5.   An alternative is to put the thumb and first finger through the hole from the outer side, grasp the end of the rope and pull it through. This works well with large holes. It is a useful skill to practise if the other method is too difficult at first.

STEP 7.   Use the second hand finger which is already through the hole as a guide.

STEP 8.   At first you will need to hold the card or ring. When the person can pull the rope through himself, you can encourage him to hold the item and to transfer his hold so that the hand that is holding the rope takes hold of the ring as the other hand pulls the rope through.

TASK ANALYSIS 6

Cuts with scissors

Goal: Can use scissors to cut pieces off a sheet of card

This activity will help the person to understand the purpose of cutting. In the early stages, beginners' loop-handled scissors or scissors with enlarged handles are best.

STEPS	Not able to cope	Has hands guided through	Can manage with prompting	Independent
1. Puts fingers in scissors, thumb uppermost				
2. Locates edge of card				
3. Opens blades of scissors by moving fingers apart				
4. Slides card between blades of scissors				
5. Squeezes scissors to cut card by moving fingers together				
6. Opens blades of scissors				
7. Slides scissors away from self				
8. Repeats Steps 5-7 until piece of card is separated				

Notes

STEP 2. Thin card, or braille writing paper, is much easier to cut than ordinary paper. Do not introduce paper until the person is competent at cutting card.

STEP 4. Teach the person to hold the card between the first finger and thumb. One blade of the scissors can then be placed against each of these to ensure that the paper is between them.

STEP 5. Teach the person to place the index finger of the cutting hand between the arms of the scissors to ensure that the blades do not close completely. If they do he will have to start from Step 2 again.

CATEGORY 1
Art and craft

Related activities

In all the activities that follow encourage the person you are teaching to do as much as possible for himself. Remember to allow him plenty of time to explore the objects he is using. Gradually reduce the amount of help you give. Do not forget to praise him for his efforts.

Natural material collage

Collect dead and green leaves and grass. Stick them all over thick paper until the paper is covered. If the person has some useful vision fasten the pictures on the wall. Join long strips of paper to make a frieze.

Tactile collage

Use materials with different textures, such as wool, corrugated cardboard, wallpaper, fabrics, bottle tops, and sandpaper. Stick them all over a large piece of paper or card.

For a change, cut the materials into pieces and stick them within an area small enough to be felt with one hand. Mark out the area with a circle of string or a cardboard "frame"

Bright collage

Materials with bright colours are especially useful for someone with residual vision. Ideas include aluminium foil, orange fluorescent paper, pieces of tinsel, large sequins, and small pieces of *Fablon*-type material with peel-off backing. This type of collage is very effective if the different materials are lined up next to each other. If they are placed at various angles, they make an interesting splash of colour.

Tile collage

Stick cork, carpet, and ceramic tiles on to a solid base of *Formica* or wood. Some tiles have a self-adhesive backing and are very easy to stick. You may want to cut large tiles into smaller shapes before using them. As they are rigid these items are easy to handle.

Pasta collage

Different shapes of pasta, and dried peas and pulses of various colours and shapes, can be stuck on to card which has had glue spread on it. Drop or press the items on to the card. They can be placed at random or within shapes outlined with string or a cardboard "frame".

Tissue pictures

Tear small pieces of tissue paper off a large sheet, crumple them up, and stick them on to backing card. There are several ways of doing this. Glue can be spread on to the pieces of tissue before pressing them on the card; glue can be spread over the backing sheet and pieces of tissue pressed on to it; pieces can be dipped in a pot of glue or paste, and then pressed on to the backing card; double-sided adhesive tape (or loops of single-sided tape) can be put on the backing card and the pieces pressed on to these. Using double-sided adhesive tape is the least messy of these methods. It is also the easiest as the tape can be located in one hand and the tissue paper pressed on to it with the other hand. You can use the completed pictures in several ways, depending on their size. They can be made into badges, cut into shapes such as trees or hens (although they will not *feel* like the real thing), made into birthday cards, or used to decorate boxes.

Sand pictures

Spread glue (PVA adhesive is ideal) over a piece of card with a brush or glue spreader. While it is still wet drop handfuls of sand on to the card to make a picture or pattern. Leave to dry.

Sandpaper pictures

Spread thick finger paint over a sheet of sandpaper using a brush, spreader, or the fingers. When dry, the paint forms smooth streaks which contrast with the roughness of the sandpaper.

Box towers

Stick plastic or cardboard containers together to make a tower. Suitable containers include chocolate boxes, margarine tubs, and cereal packets. Spread the glue with cotton buds, tooth brushes, paste spreaders, or fingers.

Decorated bottles/tubs

Cover empty tubs or bottles of different shapes and sizes with fabric. You can put the glue on the fabric directly, or on the tub or bottle.

Necklaces

Cut out small pieces of card. If these are cut off a narrow strip they will each need only one snip. Make a hole in each piece with a paper punch. String the pieces together to make a necklace or bracelet.

Cutting corrugated card

Cut the card along the grooves. Use the pieces to make a collage.

Cutting card

Glue a piece of string across some thin card from one side to the other. Cut the card into two pieces by cutting along the string with a pair of scissors. The string can form a straight line at first, but can later be curved to make the task more difficult. The shapes can be put back together like a jigsaw.

Plasticine "sausages"

Roll a lump of *Plasticine* into a sausage shape. Use it to practise cutting either with scissors or with a knife and fork. A right-handed person should hold the scissors or knife in the right hand and the fork in the left. This should be reversed for someone who is left-handed. Make sure that the implements are not too sharp and supervise the activity until the person is competent in the skill of cutting safely.

Biscuit shapes

Press *Plasticine* into a flat "cake" and use a biscuit cutter to cut out shapes. The shapes can be used for matching games or for placing back in the correct biscuit cutter. For a change use various objects to make different textured surfaces, and sort the pieces according to whether they are rough or smooth.

Thumb pots

Roll *Plasticine* into a ball about two inches in diameter. Press the thumbs into the ball to hollow out the middle. Flatten the base by pressing it on a table. Use the pots to hold a wide variety of objects.

Paper chains

Use strips of gummed paper to make a chain of interlocking loops. Alternatively, cut out strips of paper (the effect using pinking shears is pleasant to look at and to feel) and glue them into loops to form a chain. The chains can be worn round the neck or used on the wall as decorations. If the person can see use bright colours to add interest.

Balls in tin

Drop wooden balls into a metal tin. Provide a small number of balls in a tray so that the person knows how long the activity will last and draw attention to the sound of the balls as they drop. Alternatively, roll wooden or *Plasticine* balls down a tube, the end of which is placed in a tin. Listen for the sound as each ball reaches the tin. If the person is deaf, put the container on his knee. He can then feel the ball as it reaches the container.

Filling egg boxes

Use wooden balls, or make balls out of *Plasticine* or crumpled paper. Put one ball in each space. Fasten the lid of the box and shake it to hear, and feel, the balls moving inside.

Removing clothes pegs

Fasten pegs round the edge of a tin, on clothing, on a length of rope, or to each other. The person should try to find the pegs, remove them, and place them in a box. "Dolly" pegs, which can be pulled straight off, are easier to cope with than pegs with springs which have to be squeezed and then pulled. Very large paper clips can also be used for this activity.

Fastening clothes pegs

Place pegs in a box. Let the person fasten them on to the surfaces suggested above. This activity involves more dexterity than removing pegs.

Curtain rings

Use one hand to put curtain rings on the fingers of the other hand. Then shake the hand over a tin tray or box and feel or listen to the rings dropping off.

Paper beads

Cut out strips of paper about 10 inches long and one inch wide. Roll each one round a pencil and secure the ends with adhesive tape or glue. Remove them from the pencil and paint in bright colours. When dry thread string through each one to make a necklace or bracelet.

CATEGORY 2

Mobility

Task analyses

The analysed tasks given as examples in Category 2 contain the basic skills needed if someone who is blind is to be able to move around his own environment independently. It is important that these skills are taught gradually so that the person's confidence is built up with each step.

The related activities are designed to encourage movement by making it both rewarding and fun. Remember that the person may find it very frightening trying to find his way around, so give him all the help and encouragement he needs.

TASK ANALYSIS 1

Sits down

Goal: Can lower self into chair and sit acceptably

Do not try to teach this activity until you are sure that the person is able to identify the back, arms, seat, and legs of the chair.

Some people with mental and visual handicaps seem to prefer to back into chairs. The following goal, however, assumes that the person you are teaching will walk forward to the chair, and then turn to sit in it. This is a much more acceptable procedure.

STEPS	Not able to cope	Has hands guided through	Can manage with prompting	Independent
1. Locates chair				
2. Locates chair arms				
3. Sweeps hands across seat				
4. Turns round and positions self to sit down				
5. Lowers self into chair				
6. Sits acceptably in chair				

Notes

STEP 1.　When you guide the person to the chair put his hand on to the arm or the back of it rather than leaving him in front of it. He will then feel more secure as he explores with his hands to find the seat.

STEP 3.　This Step teaches the person to check that there is nothing on the seat before he sits down on it.

STEP 6.　As the person will probably never have seen anyone sitting in a chair, he may not realise how to "sit properly". Help him to understand this by letting him feel other people sitting correctly, and by moving him into a good position every time he sits down until he learns what is acceptable.

TASK ANALYSIS 2

Walks through doorways

Goal: Can negotiate a closed door by self

Doors should NEVER be left half-open if there is a possibility that someone who cannot see may bump into them. This can be very dangerous. It is important therefore that the blind person, as well as everyone else in the building, is taught always to close doors behind him.

STEPS	Not able to cope	Has hands guided through	Can manage with prompting	Independent
1. Locates door frame				
2. Checks if door is open or closed				
3. If closed, locates door knob				
4. Opens door by turning knob and pushing or pulling				
5. Walks through doorway, holding door				
6. Closes door behind him				

Notes

STEP 1.   Actually walking through an open doorway causes no difficulty. The problem is to locate the opening. Teach the person to identify door frames by feeling for the architrave and, perhaps, using sound clues.

STEP 3.   This requires a downward movement with both hands, one down each side of the door.

STEP 5.   Teach the person to keep in contact with the door rather than to let it swing open or closed. He will need to learn to transfer his grip from the inside to the outside door knob by sliding the hand round the edge of the door. It may help if the other hand holds the edge of the door steady.

STEP 6.   Although the person should be taught to close doors behind him, wherever possible try to fit doors with self-closing attachments in case he forgets to do this.

TASK ANALYSIS 3

Walks round obstacles

Goal: Can safely negotiate objects in his path and continue on his route

It is important that the person learns to cope with obstacles, such as tables, chairs, and other furniture, as these are likely to be encountered on any route he learns. Such items can provide him with useful clues as to his whereabouts. Remember, though, not to change the position of these items too often and to show him when you do. Also, remove from the environment any low obstacles that cannot be found easily with the hands.

STEPS	Not able to cope	Has hands guided through	Can manage with prompting	Independent
1. Stops on meeting obstacle				
2. Moves hand round edge of obstacle				
3. Walks forward slowly, avoiding obstacle				
4. Continues on original course				

Notes

STEP 1. Teach the person to use his hand as an effective guard. It should be held with the back facing forward, across the body (see "trailing", page 20 of this book).

STEP 2. A light touch is required for safe exploration. Refer to the section on Hand clues on page 19.

STEP 3. Teach the person to move forward slowly and carefully so that he does not push or knock over the obstacle. Encourage him to gain information from feeling with his hands. Sometimes he can use his feet to gain additional clues (see Foot clues, page 19).

STEP 4. Without a definite clue (for example, a sound to walk towards, or a strip of carpet marking the way), the person will have great difficulty relocating his route once it has been interrupted unless he is very familiar with it. Try, therefore, to keep furniture where he expects to find it, and give him plenty of help for as long as he needs it.

TASK ANALYSES OF ROUTES

Goal: Can safely find own way using familiar route

It is not possible in this book to provide detailed analyses to help you teach specific routes as every route will be unique. It is possible, however, to give you an idea of the degree of difficulty of the routes you wish to teach. You can then draw up your own analysis for each of these, making full use of available clues and the teaching techniques which have been described in Sections 2 - 5.

Begin by teaching the easiest of the routes you analyse and do not move on to the next one until the person has mastered it thoroughly. Remember also to teach each route in only one direction at a time to avoid confusion. See pp 20-22 for more information on teaching routes and pp 18-20 for the different types of clues that can be helpful.

Degree of difficulty: Easiest

The easiest routes are short, and they allow the person who is blind to remain in contact with a surface (such as a wall, table top, chairs) all the way.

Examples include: from a door to a chair which is placed against an adjoining wall; from bathroom door to toilet; from outside door along wall to a garden seat.

Degree of difficulty: Fairly easy

Such routes require some "free" travel. The distances covered are still usually quite short.

Examples include: from door across the room to own chair in the centre; from dining table across room to door; from bed to bedroom door.

Degree of difficulty: Difficult

This type of route usually covers a greater distance and is more complex for someone who cannot see. It may involve travelling between rooms, or across a large room in which there are few clues.

Examples are: from sitting room to dining room; from bedroom to bathroom; from front door to pavement; from sitting room to front door.

Summary of teaching procedure

1. Analyse the route you wish to teach, breaking it down into small sections and listing the clues in each section.

2. Guide the person through the route many times, pointing out the clues. Walk through the route in one direction only until the person can cope with it unaided. Remember, on the return journey the clues will be in a different order and additional clues or difficulties may be present. You will need to teach the return route separately.

3. Encourage the person to find clues as he comes up to them. Gradually reduce the amount of help you provide so that he has to anticipate what is coming next and must decide for himself what to do when he meets it.

4. Gradually begin to let the person walk parts of the route by himself. If one part is particularly easy, let him try that section first. He may be most interested in the last part of the route as this will take him to his goal (dining room table, own chair, tea trolley). In this case it may be best to let him start with the last part of the route.

CATEGORY 2
Mobility

Related activities

USING HAND CLUES

The following activities require the hands to be used to gather information. At first, information can be gained by using both hands clumsily. With practice the person should learn how to obtain necessary information with only a light touch by one hand. It is likely that much time will be needed to develop this skill.

Poles

Carefully hold out horizontally a lightweight pole, about six feet in length. The person finds the end of the pole and follows it with his hand until he reaches you.

Following

This is an important, "real" mobility skill. It can be practised with railings, walls, hedges, and fences. You can help the person at first by: gently holding the arm he is not using so that he feels secure; making a noise or banging the surface he is to follow to indicate where it is and encourage him to move towards it; giving him a short stick to explore with rather than his hand. This last activity is more difficult than using hands as the information gained is less precise.

String route

Tie one end of a length of string to a table, door knob, or other stationary object and stretch it out. Encourage the person to follow the string with his hand(s) until he reaches you at the other end. An extra reward when he reaches you, such as a biscuit or a drink, might maintain his interest in this. You can also add variety as he becomes more competent by stretching the string across a room, round objects in a room, between rooms, around trees, along pathways, and up and down stairs and steps.

Find the radio

Place a radio which is playing on the floor near a table. Show the person how to hold on to the edge of the table with one hand and move around it, bending over and sweeping the ground in front of him with the other hand until he finds the radio.

Skittles

Place skittles on a table. Encourage the person to try to knock them off the table with a ball and then try to find them and put them back on the table. Use the same technique to find the skittles and the ball as to find the radio in the previous example.

Crawling

The following activities allow the person to practise feeling a route with the hands, and they can be fun. You can introduce variety by placing paper bags or gloves over the person's hands. Make sure that the person understands that these activities are meant to be fun and that he should usually follow routes in an upright position! Some ideas are: through a tunnel made of chairs and blankets; under a fence or hedge; following a length of rope or string fastened on the ground. Supervise these activities carefully to make sure the person does not hurt himself. You will probably have to give him a good deal of help at first.

Table/chair maze

Arrange tables and chairs in two rows to provide a maze which ends up, perhaps, at a chair with a biscuit on it. In the early stages, the distance between the rows should be only slightly more than the width of a person. As the person's skill and confidence develops, increase this distance to make the activity more difficult. "Dead-end" pathways can also be added to make the activity more interesting. You will probably need to guide the person from item to item at first.

Table/chair route

Make up a route using only one line of tables or chairs, ending with some kind of reward. Encourage the person to feel and identify each item as he reaches it.

Musical chairs

Help the person to find his way along a row of chairs using his hands and to sit in the chair nearest to him when the music stops. When he is able to do this without help, you can gradually increase the space between the chairs. If other people join in this activity it can be more fun, but it is also more difficult as some of the chairs will be occupied.

Musical circle

A group of people hold hands in a circle. One member of the group walks round the outside of the circle, using his hand as a guide if he cannot see. When the music stops he changes places with the person closest to him. This person then goes round the circle. The sequence is repeated until all the group members have had a turn.

USING FOOT CLUES

A person who is blind can use his feet to gain useful information about where he is. This is particularly valuable on routes which offer no, or few, hand clues. The following activities will provide practice in recognising different textures and floor surfaces and help to increase self-confidence as the person learns to negotiate objects and raised surfaces.

Feels materials

You can introduce much variety in this activity, both in the materials you use and in what you do with them. Materials can include: sponge, carpet, lino, metal, smooth stones, velvet, corrugated cardboard, wood, warm water, cold water, polystyrene packing shapes, sand. (Put liquids, sand, and small items in a baby bath or large plastic bowl.) You will certainly be able to find many more. Activities could be:

1. The person sits on a chair and "plays" with the materials in bare feet. Make this interesting by covering both feet with the same material, or putting one foot in one kind of material and the other in a contrasting material. Encourage him to listen to the different sounds he makes as he moves the materials with his feet.

2. The person finds two pieces of the same material by feeling them with bare feet.

3. The person examines the materials as he feels them with his feet.

4. The person walks on the materials, both in bare feet and with shoes on. Let him start with the firmer materials (such as carpet, lino, wood) and gradually progress to those which give less support (such as sponge, sand).

Recognises surface changes

If you want the person to be able to recognise different surfaces, begin by helping him to place one foot on each of two contrasting surfaces. Practise this:

> along a strip of carpet placed on a hard surface;
>
> around the edge of large piece of hardboard placed on carpet or grass;
>
> along the kerb of a pavement to lower road edge;
>
> over grass to raised or sunken path edge;
>
> around the edge of a mattress placed on the ground.

Eventually he may be able to walk on one surface and check for the edge by moving one foot sideways, but this is much more difficult.

Follows rope or sticks

Arrange a length of rope or several sticks in a line on the ground. The person walks with one foot on each side of the rope/sticks following its direction by feeling it with the inner side of his feet. Later he could try walking on one side of it, following it by feeling sideways with one foot.

Stepping stones

Arrange objects across a surface at regular intervals. The person learns to step from one to the other without putting his feet down in between. You could use pieces of non-slip carpet at first. After he is used to this you could teach the person to step from the inside of one car tyre to the next, or between the rungs of a ladder laid on the floor.

Walks along low bench or plank

A person who is blind may feel very anxious if he moves off safe, firm ground. You MUST, therefore, be extremely careful when you introduce this activity and be prepared to offer much support and physical guidance until the person gains confidence.

Finds and avoids obstacles

Arrange obstacles, such as boxes and buckets, randomly on the floor between the person and yourself. Ask him to walk carefully to you without knocking the obstacles over or crashing noisily into them. He will have to find each one with his feet and walk around it. Speak to him or make a noise while he is doing this so that he knows where you are. This activity requires a high degree of competence.

LISTENING

A person who cannot see needs to develop listening skills in order to interpret the meaning of sounds (for example, a door bell ring) and to locate objects by sound. Begin by finding somewhere quiet to carry out the activities, where the person will not be distracted. You can introduce music or other background noises at a later stage if you want to make the tasks more difficult.

Stop the alarm

Place an alarm clock which is about to ring on a table. When the alarm sounds the person tries to find the clock before it stops ringing. For a change you could use a musical box instead.

Find the reward

Place a sweet or biscuit inside one of several containers (for example, margarine tubs) on the table. The person shakes each one in turn until he finds the one which makes a noise because it contains the reward. Let him have the reward he finds.

Spinning plates

Spin a plastic or tin plate on the table top. The person must try to find it and stop it spinning before it stops itself.

Ball in a bucket

Place a metal bucket a little in front of the person and tap it with a stick. The person tries to throw a ball into the bucket. The noise will tell him if he has succeeded. For extra fun, and providing you have a suitable place for the purpose, half fill the bucket with water and let him enjoy the splashing sound as the ball falls into the water.

Find the sound

Place a Bleep Ball, musical box, or clockwork toy some distance away from the person. His task is to find it. You can make the activity easy or difficult, depending on where you put the object.

Catch the noise

Walk around the room banging a tambourine or clapping your hands. The person must try to catch you by following the noise.

This chasing game can begin with your moving slowly away from the person in a straight line. You can gradually make it more difficult, for example, by walking in a circle. Eventually you may be able to run about anywhere in the room. You can make the game even more challenging by finding one or two other people to move about at the same time making different sounds. The person tries to find the one making the specific sound you have asked him to locate.

MOVEMENT

Mobility involves movement, that is, being able to move around *and* knowing where you are and in which direction to move. The following activities are designed to develop interest, pleasure, and confidence in the first of these skills.

Begin with the floor activities as the person who is blind is likely to feel safer with these, especially with you as his partner. When he becomes confident in items 1 - 8 you can move on to activities that require him to stand or move around.

Floor activities

1. Roll the person on the floor and encourage him to roll by himself.

2. Show the person how to stretch and curl up his body. Gradually reduce physical guidance as he learns to do this.

3. Slowly and gently rotate the person while he sits or lies on his stomach on the floor. Encourage him to rotate unaided.

5. Let the person fall sideways or backwards on to a mat or into your arms from a crouching position. Give him plenty of help at first to develop confidence in this skill.

6. Sit back to back with the person and push him gently around the floor.

7. Sit back to back with the person and push against each other. You will have to show him how to do this.

8. Sit facing the person and encourage him to push his feet against yours.

9. Stand behind or facing the person. Hold his hands or arms and sway and bend together.

10. Stand alongside the person. Each of you puts one arm around the other's waist. Walk together forwards, backwards, or sideways in rhythm and to a pattern (for example, two steps forward, one to the side).

11. Stand opposite the person. Pull or push each other.

12. Encourage the person to walk around you, remaining in contact with you all the time. Let him repeat the exercise, holding on to a chair instead of you.

Large inflatable ball

1. Help the person to push the ball against a wall, and "catch" it as it comes back. With practice he might learn to do this himself.

2. Help the person to lie on top of the ball, on his stomach or his back, and slowly roll along by moving his feet on the floor. This will encourage him to relax his body and be able to bend it at the waist. These skills are important for walking well. Be prepared to give him a great deal of help at first so that he does not become anxious when the ball begins to move.

3. Push the ball gently against the person and encourage him to push back. This will help give him a sense of balance.

4. Help the person to roll the ball. Encourage smooth flowing movement. You may need to show him how this is done many times, as he cannot learn by watching anyone else. When he is able to roll the ball and let it go, you can help him to practise by rolling it to one another.

5. Let the person lie on top of the ball on his stomach. Hold his hands and feet and gently roll him along. At first he may not like losing contact with the floor, so give him plenty of support and encouragement.

Play barrel

1. Help the person to sit on the barrel with his feet on one side of it. You may be able to encourage him to roll backwards by pushing his feet on the floor, but he will need much help at first.

2. Encourage the person to sit astride the barrel and roll from side to side, pushing each foot against the floor in turn.

3. Help the person to walk round the room pushing the barrel in front of him. Make sure that there are no obstacles in his way.

4. Ask the person to lie on his back on the floor facing a wall. Help him to roll the barrel against the wall using his feet.

Walking

1. Help the person to put each foot into a cardboard box and walk forward. This requires good balance, coordinated body movements, and careful thought about moving the feet. He will probably need support for a while. You might prefer to start with only one foot in a box.

2. Help the person to walk while balancing an object on his head or across his shoulders. He will need to learn to keep his back straight and his head erect if he is not to drop the object. Give him plenty of practice. You will have to hold the object lightly in place at first.

Tyre on castors

1. Sit the person on the tyre. Encourage him to push himself round.

2. Sit the person on the tyre. Hold his feet and pull him along.

3. Sit the person on the tyre with a rope or hoop around his waist. Teach him to hold on to the rope or hoop with both hands as you pull him along.

CATEGORY 3

Housecraft

Task analyses

Category 3 contains example task analyses of some everyday practical skills which you can use to increase the person's independence in a familiar setting.

You should expect and encourage the person who is blind to participate as fully as possible in the day to day routine of his own environment. Do not let him sit passively on the sidelines. If you help him to play an active part, he will gradually be able to make more sense of his surroundings and what is happening to him or near him.

TASK ANALYSIS 1

Places table mats on table

Goal: Can place mats in appropriate position on table

This analysis assumes that one table mat is to be placed on the table for each person. It is best to begin learning with rectangular mats as their shape makes it easier to recognise where to put them and where the necessary cutlery will be arranged. Circular mats can be introduced later. *Dycem* non-slip mats are excellent for holding plates in position but are more difficult to arrange on the table as they have to be lifted, rather than slid, into position.

STEPS	Not able to cope	Has hands guided through	Can manage with prompting	Independent
1. Carries mats to table				
2. Stands directly behind chair				
3. Places first mat on table				
4. Lines up long edge of mat with edge of table				
5. Lines up short edges of mat centrally in front of chair				

Notes

STEP 3.   If the person has carried several mats he should put them in a pile on the table. He should then pick up each mat from the pile, one at a time, and place it correctly on the table. To begin with it might be easier if he hands you the pile and takes them from you one at a time.

STEP 4.   The person can achieve this step by holding his thumbs on the table edge in front of him and lining up the long edge of the mat so that it just touches the tips of his thumbs.

STEP 5.   The person leans over the back of the chair with one arm on each side of it and his hands touching the table. This gives an indication of the correct position for the mat. You will probably need to help him with this step for quite a long time by guiding his hands first to the table and then to find the mat and move it between his hands centrally in front of him.

TASK ANALYSIS 2

Places cutlery on table

Goal: Can place cutlery correctly around a place mat

This analysis assumes that a knife, fork, and spoon are to be used. It can be easily adjusted for other combinations of cutlery. When the person is competent at placing cutlery around a rectangular mat you can introduce a circular mat and a plate. Teach him to place the plate on top of the mat using the same procedure as for the mat itself.

STEPS	Not able to cope	Has hands guided through	Can manage with prompting	Independent
1. Picks out a knife, fork, and spoon from the cutlery tray				
2. Identifies fork and puts in left hand				
3. Places fork in line with left-hand edge of mat				
4. Identifies knife and holds in right hand (transfers spoon to left hand if necessary)				
5. Places knife in line with right-hand edge of mat				
6. Transfers spoon to right hand				
7. Places spoon in line with back edge of mat				

Notes

STEP 1. Keep knives, forks, and spoons on a tray or in a compartmentalised box until they are needed. When learning which items of cutlery are needed at a place setting, it is best to collect all the necessary pieces for one place in the hand at the start and to lay them correctly on the table. Then return to the tray for sufficient pieces for the next place setting.

STEP 3. The right hand feels for the edge of the mat and acts as a guide while the left hand places the fork alongside.

STEP 5. Again, both hands are needed. The left hand feels for the edge of the mat, while the right places the knife in the correct position.

STEP 6. It may be easier to place the spoon facing in the correct direction if it is held in the right hand. The left hand can be used if preferred. The important thing is for the same hand, whether right or left, to be used on every occasion so that the person does not become confused about which way round to hold the spoon.

TASK ANALYSIS 3

Stacks empty plates and cutlery after meal

Goal: Can stack empty plates on top of one another and put cutlery on top plate

This task becomes more difficult as the number of plates on the pile increases and each new plate has to be lifted higher to be placed on the top. Three or four plates is probably the maximum that should be attempted. Make the task easier at first by holding the cutlery until the person is ready to place it on the top of the pile.

It is assumed that all the plates are empty. If food has been left on a plate, the task is much more difficult and the person is likely always to need help.

STEPS	Not able to cope	Has hands guided through	Can manage with prompting	Independent
1. Places first plate in front of self				
2. Locates and moves second plate alongside first				
3. Relocates first plate				
4. Locates cutlery on first plate				
5. Picks up cutlery				
6. Puts cutlery on second plate				
7. Picks up second plate				
8. Slides second plate on top of first plate to start pile				

Notes

STEP 2. If the person holds the second plate with both hands on the edge, he can slide it along the table until he feels the first plate with the back of the fingers of one hand.

STEP 4. The person puts both hands together in front of him and then moves them in opposite directions round the outside edge of the plate to find all the cutlery.

STEPS 5 and 6. This method is easier than trying to lift and balance a heavy pile of plates with cutlery on top.

STEP 7. This is a difficult step, as the person must hold the plate level if the cutlery is not to fall off. It is best to put his fingers under the plate and his thumbs on top. The thumbs can be used to steady the cutlery.

TASK ANALYSIS 4

Hangs own coat on peg

Goal: Can hang coat by the loop over a peg

This activity can be made simpler if you teach the person to take off his coat carefully so that it is easier for him to find the loop. To do this, show him how to remove the first arm from its sleeve by pulling the sleeve with his other hand. He must then let go of the first sleeve and pull the second sleeve slowly off the second arm with the other hand. As the hand comes out of the top of the sleeve he slides it carefully along the edge of the coat until it reaches the collar.

STEPS	Not able to cope	Has hands guided through	Can manage with prompting	Independent
1. Finds loop				
2. Holds coat by loop with one hand				
3. Locates hanging peg with other hand				
4. Lifts coat loop over peg				

Notes

STEP 2. If the person holds the second plate with both hands on the edge, he can slide it along the table until he feels the first plate with the back of the fingers of one hand.

STEP 4. The person puts both hands together in front of him and then moves them in opposite directions round the outside edge of the plate to find all the cutlery.

STEPS 5 and 6. This method is easier than trying to lift and balance a heavy pile of plates with cutlery on top.

STEP 7. This is a difficult step, as the person must hold the plate level if the cutlery is not to fall off. It is best to put his fingers under the plate and his thumbs on top. The thumbs can be used to steady the cutlery.

TASK ANALYSIS 5

Lifts own coat off peg

Goal: Can lift own coat off peg

You can help the person to identify his own clothes by drawing attention to "clues" provided by the design of the garment, such as flaps on a pocket, fur lining to anorak hood, or a quilted lining. Guide his hand to find these until he is familiar with them.

If possible provide enough pegs to allow for only one garment to be hung on each peg. This will make it easier for the person to find and remove his own coat.

STEPS	Not able to cope	Has hands guided through	Can manage with prompting	Independent
1. Locates coat				
2. Locates loop of coat				
3. Locates peg with other hand				
4. Lifts coat off peg (upwards and towards self)				

Notes

STEPS 1 and 2. If necessary you can add extra clues to help the person find his own belongings, for example, a velvet rectangle or a large button sewn inside the collar which match the clues you have used to mark his peg. Once he has found the identification clue guide his hands to find the loop.

STEP 3. The person should hold on to his coat with one hand and move the other hand upwards to find the peg. Let the person use the same peg for his coat every time until he is very familiar with it. Occasionally you may wish to change his peg to provide a fresh challenge.

STEP 4. You must emphasise the lifting aspect of this movement. Move the person's fingers upwards along the stem of the peg until the coat can be lifted off. If not, the person is likely to pull the garment downwards, breaking the loop or loosening the peg.

TASK ANALYSIS 6

Fastens buttons

Goal: Can fasten large buttons on coat

In the following analysis, for women the first hand is the right hand and the second hand is the left hand. This is reversed for men because of the way their garments fasten.

STEPS	Not able to cope	Has hands guided through	Can manage with prompting	Independent
1. Locates buttonhole with first hand				
2. Pushes index finger of first hand through hole				
3. Locates and holds button with second hand				
4. Puts edge of button next to tip of first hand index finger				
5. Pushes button along index finger and into hole				
6. Grasps button with first hand				
7. Pulls button through hole				

Notes

STEP 2. This finger will act as a guide to the location of the hole. If the index finger and the thumb can be pushed through the hole, the task will be easier as they can grasp the button and pull it through.

STEP 3. The best way to ensure that it is the right button is to start at the top of the coat and work down.

STEP 5. Slide the edge of the button along the finger and through the buttonhole.

STEP 6. The thumb and index finger of the first hand grasp the edge of the button and then the second hand lets it go.

STEP 7. While the button is being pulled through, the second hand can hold the edge of the material near the buttonhole so that the button moves through the hole more easily. Alternatively, the thumb of the second hand can push the button while it is being pulled from the other side.

CATEGORY 3

Housecraft

Related activities

Using pegs

Scissors, cups, keys on rings, hoops, bags and other items can all be kept tidily, and can easily be found, if routinely hung on pegs. Let the person practise this skill with various items and encourage him to return each item he uses to its peg when he has finished with it. Tidiness is particularly important for someone who cannot see as he will find it very difficult to find an item that has been misplaced.

Pop on beads

Make chains, necklaces, or bracelets with large plastic beads which pull apart and push together. Pull them apart dropping each one into a tin box or bucket. Putting them together again requires a movement very similar to pushing a button through a buttonhole.

Stacking

Place several yoghurt tubs, paper plates, or similar items separately on the table. Show the person how to find them one at a time and then stack one on top of the other. When he is used to this, make the task more difficult by putting a small object inside some of the tubs or on a few of the plates. Ask the person to check that each item is empty before stacking it. This is good practice for clearing the dining table after meals and will teach the person to look for cutlery before stacking. Do not expect him, however, to be able to cope with plates which still contain food.

Tidying up

Scatter magazines or books on tables and chairs around the room. Let the person find them and pile them up neatly on a table or put them on a bookshelf.

Fitting shapes

Put sticks into a sorting tray which has both horizontal and vertical compartments. The sticks have to be turned in the right direction to fit in the tray. This is good practice for putting away cutlery.

If the person needs further practice in the skill of turning shapes round to fit into holes you can use inset form boards. Remember, however, that if the person cannot see many of the shapes used will not help him to recognise the real objects they represent (such as farmyard animals, trees, furniture) as they will be the wrong size, will not smell the same, will not move, and will not be the right texture. Using the form board, therefore, will only help him learn to fit shapes appropriately.

Sorting

Give the person a few knifes, forks, spoons, plates, dishes, cups or other everyday utensils. It is best to start with only two kinds at first. Show him how to feel the different shapes and sizes to identify them and then place them in separate containers or compartments.

You can teach him to sort items of clothing and household linen in the same way. For a change, cut out squares of different materials (wool, cotton, velvet, fur, hessian, lace, silk, towelling, PVC). Show the person how to sort them into boxes or paper bags.

CATEGORY 4
Food and drink

Task analyses

The analyses given in Category 4 have been chosen because they can be used to teach the basic skills that the person will need in order to be able to prepare simple items of food and drink.

Try to ensure that the refreshments prepared are usually enjoyed by the person you are teaching. If so, the end product of each task should act as an incentive to learning.

TASK ANALYSIS 1
Pours from a jug

Goal: Can pour a drink from a jug

This basic sequence can be used for all pouring activities using various containers and liquids. If saucers are to be used, or if the person is to carry a cup full of liquid, extra steps will have to be added to teach the necessary skills.

STEPS	Not able to cope	Has hands guided through	Can manage with prompting	Independent
1. Locates cup with one hand				
2. Locates jug with other hand				
3. Moves jug next to cup				
4. Lines up spout with cup				
5. Pours liquid into cup				
6. Stops pouring when sufficient liquid is in cup				
7. Returns jug to appropriate position				
8. Lifts up cup to drink				

Notes

STEP 1.   The person identifies the cup, moves it in front of himself, and steadies it with one hand.

STEP 3.   The person may find it easier to slide the jug across the surface with the other hand rather than to try to lift it into the air. If so, teach him to check that the way is clear first by feeling the area between the cup and the jug with the hand that is going to move the jug.

STEP 4.   Teach the person to span the top of the cup with the thumb and middle finger of one hand while the first finger points upwards to contact the spout or pouring lip of the jug.

STEP 6.   One way is to place the tip of the first finger over the rim of cup so that the finger-tip comes into contact with the liquid as the cup becomes full.

TASK ANALYSIS 2

Makes drink with powder and liquid

Goal: Can make a drink using powder and liquid

This task consists of three parts. The first part (Steps 1-16) involves putting the powder into the cup. The second part (Steps 17-22) uses the basic pouring sequence learned in Analysis 1. The third part (Steps 23-26) involves mixing the powder and liquid together.

STEPS	Not able to cope	Has hands guided through	Can manage with prompting	Independent
1. Locates cup				
2. Locates spoon				
3. Locates jar of powder				
4. Moves jar next to cup				
5. Unscrews lid from jar				
6. Places lid on surface				
7. Holds spoon correct way up				
8. Places spoon in powder				
9. Lifts filled spoon out of powder				
10. Relocates cup				
11. Moves spoon to cup				
12. Puts powder in cup by tilting spoon				
13. Puts spoon in cup				
14. Locates jar top				
15. Screws top on to jar				
16. Replaces jar in appropriate position				
17. Locates jug				
18. Moves jug next to cup				
19. Lines up spout with cup				
20. Pours liquid into cup				
21. Stops pouring when sufficient liquid is in cup				
22. Returns jug to appropriate position				
23. Locates spoon				
24. Stirs drink with spoon				
25. Places spoon in appropriate position				
26. Lifts up cup to drink				

Notes

STEP 2.   The spoon can be placed inside the empty cup so that it is easy to find again.

(continued overleaf)

STEP 6. The lid should be put down where it can easily be found (for example, in contact with the jar, on the edge of the table, or next to a pile of saucers).

STEP 7. This can be achieved by feeling the bowl of the spoon.

STEP 11. It may help to have one hand under the bowl of the spoon to avoid spilling powder on the table. Alternatively, the person may find it more helpful to use one hand to hold the cup so that he does not have to search for it again.

STEPS 13-22. If the spoon is left in the cup, it will be easier to relocate later in the task but one hand should hold the cup throughout the pouring sequence so that it is not knocked over.

TASK ANALYSIS 3

Pours cup of tea

Goal: Given the ingredients, can pour a cup of tea

This analysis is a combination of the two previous analyses and shows how a combination of the skills learned can be used together to provide a method of carrying out quite a complex activity.

If sugar is used extra steps will need to be added to take account of this and also to set a procedure for finding and using a teaspoon.

STEPS	Not able to cope	Has hands guided through	Can manage with prompting	Independent
1. Locates saucer and puts in front of self				
2. Locates cup				
3. Puts cup on saucer				
4. Locates milk jug				
5. Lines up milk jug spout with cup				
6. Pours correct amount of milk into cup				
7. Moves jug back to original location				
8. Locates teapot				
9. Lines up teapot spout with cup				
10. Pours correct amount of tea				
11. Replaces teapot in position				
12. Lifts up cup to drink				

Notes

STEP 6. If the person puts his little finger down inside the cup and pours the milk until it just touches his finger tip, he will be able to measure the correct amount of milk.

TASK ANALYSIS 4

Spreads margarine

Goal: Can spread margarine evenly over a slice of bread

The analysis describes spreading margarine, but it can be applied to any other similar food, such as pastes, jams, and spreads. The steps written assume the person is right handed. They will need to be reversed for a left-handed person.

STEPS	Not able to cope	Has hands guided through	Can manage with prompting	Independent
1. Locates knife				
2. Locates margarine				
3. Places knife edge on top of margarine				
4. Scrapes knife across margarine				
5. Repeats scraping movement several times				
6. Locates slice of bread				
7. Places knife on far corner of bread				
8. Slides knife across far edge of bread, spreading margarine				
9. Locates far corner of bread				
10. Places knife on far corner of bread				
11. Slides knife towards self, spreading margarine				
12. Repeats this movement, moving knife sideways across bread				
13. Turns bread through 180°				
14. Repeats Steps 10-12				

Notes

STEP 1. The knife should be held with the first finger resting on the back of the blade.

STEP 3. If the thumb and middle finger of the hand holding the container are stretched across the top of it, the back of the knife blade can rest against the middle finger as it is guided into the margarine.

STEP 5. Step 5 can be omitted if the item to be spread is very soft.

STEP 7. For right-handed people, this should be the far left-hand corner.

STEP 8. The back of the thumb can be used to guide the hand along the far edge of the bread.

STEP 11. Again, the back of the thumb can serve as a guide along the left hand side edge of the bread.

STEP 12. For each downward movement, the knife is moved further towards the right hand side of the bread.

STEPS 13, 14. If Step 12 is carried out precisely, the margarine may already be spread adequately and these Steps can be omitted.

TASK ANALYSIS 5

Slices bread with knife

Goal: Can slice bread with a knife

This analysis is also suitable for slicing other kinds of food, such as cake, fruit, vegetables, and cheese. Supervise this activity very carefully until the person is very competent.

STEPS	Not able to cope	Has hands guided through	Can manage with prompting	Independent
1. Locates knife				
2. Holds knife ready for cutting				
3. Locates bread on board				
4. Finds top of bread				
5. Places knife on top of bread				
6. Moves knife downwards away from self				
7. Returns knife towards self				
8. Repeats steps 6 and 7 until knife has cut through to board				
9. Stops cutting				
10. Places knife on table				

Notes

STEP 2. Probably the easiest way is to hold the knife with the end of the handle in the palm of the hand, and the first finger extended down the back of the blade.

STEP 3. It is advisable to put the bread on a board so that the table top will not be damaged.

STEP 3. One hand holds the bread, with one finger extended to act as a guide.

STEP 6. The person presses down on the knife as it moves away from him.

STEP 7. If the person has difficulty returning the knife towards him, he can lift it out of the bread completely and start the procedure again from Step 4.

TASK ANALYSIS 6

Peels fruit

Goal: Can remove the skin from a banana

This analysis can also be applied to peeling oranges and grapefruit but as the skins are much more difficult to remove the task is also more difficult.

STEPS	Not able to cope	Has hands guided through	Can manage with prompting	Independent
1. Locates banana				
2. Places banana on plate in front of self				
3. Locates knife				
4. Holds knife ready for cutting				
5. Locates end of banana				
6. Cuts through end of banana				
7. Replaces knife on table				
8. Picks up banana with one hand				
9. Locates cut end of skin with other hand				
10. Pulls skin off banana				
11. Places piece of skin on plate				
12. Repeats Steps 9-11				

Notes

STEP 4. The best way to hold the knife is with the end of the handle in the palm of the hand, and the first finger extended down the back of the blade.

STEP 6. This step is difficult, and requires much practice. Give the person plenty of help to master this as it makes peeling very much easier.

CATEGORY 4
Food and drink

Related activities

Some of the following activities do not involve food and drink. They are included here because they provide useful opportunities to practise many of the skills required in the preparation of food.

Fruit squash

Mix the concentrate with water. The person may find it fun to use warm, previously boiled water, adding ice cubes and listening to the cracking sounds.

Milk shakes

Several fruit flavoured powders are available which can be mixed with milk. You may be able to show the person how to use a hand whisk, or help him to do so. This can alter the consistency and add bubbles to provide variety and fun.

Chocolate drop sandwich

Spread two slices of bread and cover one slice with chocolate drops. Place the second slice on top to make a sandwich. This sandwich is very simple to make. To make it more difficult, see if the person can break each drop in half first.

Banana sandwich

Spread two slices of bread. Peel a banana and slice it with a knife. Place pieces on one slice of bread and put the other on top.

For a change mix a small amount of milk with the banana and mash it with a fork. Spread the mixture over the bread with a knife.

Cheese slice sandwich

Spread bread. Place a slice of processed cheese on one slice. Put second slice on top.

Cheese sandwich

Grate cheese on to a plate. Carefully remove grater. Spread two slices of bread. Fill tablespoon with grated cheese and tip on to first slice. Spread out. Place second slice on top.

Open sandwiches

For a change you can sometimes use crispbreads, crackers, or toast instead of bread. These offer a variety of interesting textures and flavours, but preparing them requires finer control than is needed when using bread.

Cold dessert

Mix as directed on the packet. Decorate with slices of fruit, chocolate buttons, or sponge fingers.

Celery and apple

Cut apple quarters into slices. Slice celery into small chunks. Mix together to make a salad. This requires the use of a fairly sharp knife. Supervise the task at all stages.

Spooning sand

Put spoonfuls of sand into a bucket. Hold one hand under the spoon to check whether the sand is being spilt. This is good practice for spooning the powders used in drinks or sugar if it is used.

Carrying pegs

Place small plastic pegboard pegs in a container. Use a spoon to transfer them from the container into small plastic tubs. This is good practice for spooning food of various kinds from serving dishes on to plates or fruit bowls. Alternatively pour the pegs from a jug into the tubs to practise the skill of pouring. As long as he is not deaf the person will be able to hear whether he has succeeded by the clattering sound. If he is deaf he will have to feel inside the tubs with his fingertips.

Bicycle wheels

Using a bicycle upside down, the person turns the back wheel by moving one of the pedals round by hand. Steady the bicycle to ensure it does not tip over. The person can feel or listen to the wheel going round. Supervise this activity throughout to make certain he does not trap his fingers. This circular movement is similar to the one used when stirring and mixing.

Sources of further information

General

ACE (Aids to Communication in Education Centre)
Mrs. P. Fuller, Ormeród School, Wayneflete Road, Headington,
Oxford OX3 8DD — 0865 635508

Action for the Disabled Association
26 Barker Walk, Mount Ephraim Road, Streatham, London SW16 — 01-677 1276

British Deaf Association
38 Victoria Place, Carlisle CA1 1HU — 0228 20188

British Institute of Mental Handicap Information and Resource Centre
Wolverhampton Road, Kidderminster, Worcs. DY10 3PP — 0562 850251

British Talking Book Service for the Blind
Mount Pleasant, Wembley, Middlesex HA0 1RR — 01-903 6666

Centre on Environment for the Handicapped
126 Albert Street, London NW1 7NF — 01-267 6111

Communication Aids Centres (England and Wales)
Boulton Road, West Bromwich, Birmingham — 021-553 0908
Castle Farm Road, Newcastle-upon-Tyne — 091-284 0480
Charing Cross Hospital, Fulham Palace Road, London W6 — 01-748 2040
Frenchay Hospital, Bristol BS16 1LE — 0272 565656
Roakwood Hospital, Fairwater Road, Llandaff, Cardiff — 0222 566281
The Wolfson Centre, Mecklenburgh Square, London WC1N 2AP — 01-837 7618

Disability Alliance ERA,
25 Denmark Street, London WC2H 8NJ — 01-240 0806

Disabled Living Foundation
380/384 Harrow Road, London W9 2HU — 01-289 6111

Down's Children's Association
4 Oxford Street, London W1N 9FL — 01-580 0511

Equipment for the Disabled
Mary Marlborough Lodge, Nuffield Orthopaedic Centre, Headington,
Oxford OX3 7LD — 0865 750103

Free Tape Recorded Library for the Blind
26 Laggan Road, Maidenhead, Berks. SL6 7JZ — 0628 20014

In Touch
10 Norman Road, Sale, Cheshire M33 3DF — 061-962 4441

National Autistic Society
276 Willesden Lane, London NW2 5RB
01-451 3844

National Children's Bureau
8 Wakley Street, London EC1V 7QE
01-278 9441

National Deaf Children's Society
31 Gloucester Place, London W1H 4EA
01-229 9272

Royal Association for Disability and Rehabilitation (RADAR)
25 Mortimer Street, London W1N 8AB
01-637 5400

Royal National Institute for the Blind (The)
224 Great Portland Street, London W1N 6AA
01-388 1266

Royal National Institute for the Deaf (The)
105 Gower Street, London WC1E 6AH
01-387 8033

Royal Society for Mentally Handicapped Children and Adults
Mencap National Centre, 123 Golden Lane, London EC1Y 0RT
01-253 9433

Sense — The National Deaf-Blind and Rubella Association
311 Gray's Inn Road, London WC1X 8PT
01-278 1005

Special Families Centre
Sunley House, Gunthorpe Street, London E1 6LS
01-247 1416

The Southern and Western Regional Association for the Blind
55 Eton Avenue, London NW3 3ET
01-222 8843

The Spastics Society
12 Park Crescent, London W1N 4EQ
01-636 5020

Toy Libraries Association
Wyllyotts Manor, Darkes Lane, Potters Bar, Herts. EN6 2HL
0707 44571

Sign/symbol systems

Amer-Ind Code
Semed Inc.
36100 Genesee Lake Road, Oconomawoe, Wisconsin, USA
Mrs. S. D. Leavesley, 52 Marston Road, Stafford ST16 3BU
0785 56231

Blissymbolics
Blissymbolics Communication Institute
350 Rumsey Road, Toronto, Canada M4G 1R8
Blissymbolics Communication Resource Centre (UK)
South Glamorgan Institute of Higher Education, Western Avenue,
Llandaff, Cardiff CF5 2YB
0222 551770

British Sign Language
Council for the Advancement of Communication with Deaf People
Pelaw House, School of Education, University of Durham, Leazes Road,
Durham DH1 1TA
0385 43611

Sign Language Project
School of Education Research Unit, University of Bristol, 19 Berkeley Square, Bristol BS8 1HS

Cued Speech
National Centre for Cued Speech
68 Upper Richmond Road, London SW15 2RP   01-870 5335

Makaton Vocabulary
Makaton Vocabulary Development Project
31 Firwood Drive, Camberley, Surrey GU15 3QD   0276 61390

Paget-Gorman Signed Speech
Paget-Gorman Society
3 Gipsy Lane, Headington, Oxford OX3 7PT   0865 61908

Rebus
Oakwood School
Druid's Walk, Walsall Wood, Walsall, West Midlands WS9 9JS   0543 375044

Suppliers of aids and equipment

Antiference Ltd., Bicester Road, Aylesbury, Bucks.
Manoy easy-grip cutlery and lightweight break-resistant melamine tablewear.

BSG International (Britax-Excelsior) Ltd., Chertsey Road, Byfleet, Weybridge, Surrey KT14 7AW
Car safety seats in two sizes and body harnesses.

Deron Electronics Ltd., Unit 7, Foundry Lane, Byker, Newcastle-upon-Tyne, 6.
A range of electronic toys and teaching aids.

Dycem Plastics Ltd., Ashley Hill Trading Estate, Bristol, BS2 9XS
Dycem non-slip pads and mats.

ESA Creative Learning Ltd., Esavian Works, Fairview Road, Stevenage SG1 QNX
A large range of learning materials.

Hestair Hope Ltd., St. Philip's Drive, Royston, Oldham, OL2 6AG
A large range of learning materials.

Huntercraft, The Castle House, Sherborne, Dorset DT9 3BU
A large range of learning materials.

LDA (Learning Development Aids), Duke Street, Wisbech, Cambs. PE13 2AE
A large range of learning materials.

Newton Aids Ltd., Unit 4, Dolphin Industrial Estate, Southampton Road, Salisbury, Wilts.
Two-handled beaker with large handles for older children and adults.

Nomeq, Nottingham Handcraft Ltd., 17 Ludlow Hill Road, Melton Road, West Bridgford, Nottingham.
Children's furniture; *Manoy* plates and cutlery; *Dycem* non-slip mats; *Rubazote* — for enlarging handles of cutlery to give easier grip.

Phonic Ear Inc., 250 Camino Alto, Mill Valley, California, CA 94941

Possum Controls Ltd., Middlegreen Road, Langley, Berks. SL3 6DF.
Electronic learning, communication, and information systems; large play/rehabilitation equipment.

The Spastics Society, 16 Fitzroy Square, London W1P 5HQ.
Aids and equipment information service; exhibition of equipment; production of a variety of aids.

Toys for the Handicapped, 76 Barracks Road, Sandy Lane Industrial Estate, Stourport-on-Severn, Worcs. DY13 9QB.
Exciting well-designed indoor and outdoor equipment suitable for children and adults.

Werth, P. C. Ltd., 45 Nightingale Lane, London SW12 8SU.
Hearing aids and full range of audiometry equipment.

Recommended reading

Ellis, D. (Ed.). *Sensory impairments in mentally handicapped people.* London: Croom Helm, 1986.

Freeman, P. *The deaf/blind baby: a programme of care.* London: Heinemann Medical Books, 1985.

Information Exchange. Newsletter of the Royal National Institute for the Blind, London.

Longhorn, F. *Planning a sensory curriculum.* Northampton: Wren Spinney School, 1985.

McInnes, J., Treffry, J. *Deaf/blind infants and children.* Milton Keynes: Open University, 1982.

Royal National Institute for the Blind. *How to guide a blind person.* London: RNIB (undated).

Simon, G. B. (Ed.). *The next step on the ladder — assessment and management of children with multiple handicaps (4th edition).* Kidderminster: BIMH Publications, 1986.

Talking Sense. Newsletter of Sense — The National Deaf-Blind and Rubella Association, London.

The Disability Rights Handbook. London: Disability Alliance ERA (annual).

Wyman, R. *Multiply handicapped children.* London: Souvenir Press, 1986.

Further reading

Balthazar, E. E. *Balthazar scales of adaptive behavior.* Windsor: NFER/Nelson, 1981.

Bluma, S., Shearer, M., Frohman, A., Hilliard, J. *Portage guide to early education.* Windsor: NFER/Nelson, 1976.

Buckley, A. *Developing senses. A practical guide to creative group work.* London: PARVO, C/o CBEVE, Semour Mews, W1H 9PE.

Conacher, G. (Ed.). *Kitchen sense for disabled people.* London: Croom Helm, 1986.

Deich, R. F., Hodges, P. M. *Language without speech.* London: Souvenir Press, 1977.

Freeman, P. *Understanding the deaf/blind child.* London: Heinemann, 1975.

Gardner, J. M., Murphy, J. W., Crawford, N. B. *The skills analysis model — an effective curriculum for children with severe learning difficulties.* Kidderminster: BIMH Publications, 1983.

Golding, R., Goldsmith, L. *The caring person's guide to handling the severely multiply handicapped.* London: Macmillan, 1986.

Gunzburg, H. C. *Progress assessment chart.* Stratford-on-Avon: SEFA Publications. Available from: London: RSMHCA.

Hogg, J., Sebba, J. *Profound retardation and multiple impairment: Vol. 2 — education and theory.* London: Croom Helm, 1986.

Jones, P. R., Cregan, A. *Sign and symbol communication for mentally handicapped people.* London: Croom Helm, 1986.

Kiernan, C., Reid, B., Jones, L. *Signs and symbols: use of non-vocal communication systems.* London: Heinemann Educational Books, 1982.

McCartney, E. *Helping adult training centre students to communicate.* Kidderminster: BIMH Publications, 1984.

Maxfield, K. E., Buchholz, F. *Scale of social maturity for use with pre-school blind children.* New York: American Foundation for the Blind Inc., 1957.

Mencap (SW). *Emotional responses of mentally handicapped people. (Report of the 16th RSMHCA Spring Conference.)* Taunton: Mencap South West Region, 1983.

Myklebust, H. R. *The psychology of deafness, sensory deprivation, learning and adjustment.* London: Grune and Stratton, 1964.

Nihira, K. *AAMD Adaptive Behavior Scale.* Washington: American Association on Mental Deficiency, 1974.

Nolan, M., Tucker, I. G. *The hearing-impaired child and the family.* London: Souvenir Press, 1981.

Perkins, E. A., Taylor, P. D., Capie, A. C. M. *Developmental Checklist (2nd edn.).* Kidderminster: BIMH Publications, 1980.

Perkins, E. A., Taylor, P. D., Capie, A. C. M. *Helping people learn. (Helping the retarded 3rd revised edn.).* Kidderminster: BIMH Publications *(in press).*

Presland, J. L. *Paths to mobility in "special care": a guide to teaching gross motor skills to very handicapped children.* Kidderminster: BIMH Publications, 1982.

Reed, M. *Educating hearing-impaired children.* Milton Keynes: Open University, 1984.

Reynell, J. K. *Reynell developmental language scales.* Windsor: NFER/Nelson, 1977.

RNIB. *Catalogue of RNIB aids and games.* London: RNIB (annual).

RNID. *Services and information leaflet.* London: RNID.

RNID. *Sign and say.* London: RNID, 1981.

Sebba, J. *Visual checklist.* Manchester: Univ. Manchester Hester Adrian Research Centre, 1978.

Sidle, N. *Rubella in pregnancy. A review of rubella as an infection in pregnancy, its consequences and prevention.* London: Sense, 1985.

Simon, G. B. *The NSL developmental assessment scale.* Kidderminster, BIMH Publications, 1982.

Taylor, P. D., Robinson, P. *Crossing the road — a guide to teaching the mentally handicapped.* Kidderminster: BIMH Publications, 1979.

Thorpe, S. *Designing for people with sensory impairments.* London: CEH, 1986.

Wechsler, D. *Wechsler adult intelligence scale.* New York: Psychol. Corp., 1955.

Wilson, G., Murphy, B. (Eds.). *Self-injurious behaviour: a collection of published papers on prevalence, causes, and treatment in people who are mentally handicapped or autistic.* Kidderminster: BIMH Publications, 1985.

Wood, M. *Music for living — enriching the lives of profoundly mentally handicapped people.* Kidderminster, BIMH Publications, 1982.

Yule, W., Carr, J. *Behaviour modification for the mentally handicapped.* London: Croom Helm, 1980.

Index